Getting Started in Science

Experiments with
Light and Mirrors

Robert Gardner

ENSLOW PUBLISHERS, INC.

44 Fadem Road	P.O. Box 38
Box 699	Aldershot
Springfield, N.J. 07081	Hants GU12 6BP
U.S.A.	U.K.

Library of Congress Cataloging-in-Publication Data

Gardner, Robert, 1929–
    Experiments with light and mirrors / Robert Gardner.
        p. cm. — (Getting started in science)
    Includes bibliographical references and index.
    ISBN 0-89490-668-2
    1. Light—Experiments—Juvenile literature. 2. Mirrors—
Experiments—Juvenile literature. 3. Reflection (Optics)—
Experiments—Juvenile literature. [1. Light—Experiments.
2. Mirrors—Experiments. 3. Reflection (Optics)—Experiments.
4. Experiments.] I. Title. II. Series: Gardner, Robert, 1929–
Getting started in science.
QC360.G368 1995
535.2'078—dc20

                        95-12219
                           CIP
                           AC

Printed in the United States of America

10 9 8 7 6 5 4 3 2 1

Illustration Credits: Kimberly Austin Daly.

Cover Photo: Comstock, Inc.

Contents

Introduction

When you hear the word mirror, you may think of your-self because you see yourself in mirrors. Actually, what you see in a mirror is an *image* of yourself; it is not really you. However, every magician knows that people can be tricked into believing that images are the real thing.

Mirrors can be found in many places. You see them in bathrooms, bedrooms, living rooms, corridors and hallways, and dance studios; on the sides of cars, trucks, and buses; in periscopes, telescopes, and mi-croscopes; in barber shops and beauty salons; in fun houses; and in makeup kits. Just about anywhere you look, you will find mirrors. What you may not realize is that mirrors can also serve as a pathway to science.

In this book, mirrors are used for experiments—ex-periments you can do in sunlight, shade, and even darkness. You will use a mirror to write in a different way and read print that appears to be illegible. You will carry out experiments that involve the reflection of light, col-ored light, and sunlight. You will investigate different kinds of mirrors and see how light can be reflected in a variety of ways.

Experiments with Mirrors will allow you to carry out experiments using mirrors and other simple materials more often associated with play than with science. These experiments will lead you to a number of scien-tific discoveries, principles, puzzlers, and surprises. They will help you to learn how science works, because you will be investigating the world as scientists do.

Some experiments will be preceded by an explanation of a scientific principle. Once you understand the basic idea, you should have enough information to allow you to answer questions and interpret results in the experiments that come after the principle. Some of these experiments might start you on a path leading to a science fair project.

A few puzzlers and surprises related to the experiments are scattered throughout the book. The answers to these puzzlers and surprises can be found by doing more experiments or by turning to the back of the book. But don't turn to the answers right away. See if you can come up with your own solutions to the problems and questions first. Then compare your answers with the ones given.

The experiments and activities included in this book were chosen because they can be investigated with mirrors. Most of them are safe and can be done without expensive equipment. If an experiment requires the use of a knife, a flame, or anything that has a potential for danger, you will be asked to work with an adult. Please do so! The purpose of such a request is to protect you from getting hurt.

It is likely that humans first viewed their own images by gazing at the surface of very still water in a puddle, lake, or pond. As you look more closely at light, mirrors, and reflections, you will find "mirrors" in unexpected places—in glass doors and windows, in the shiny fender of a car, in television screens, door knobs, and mud puddles. Be on the lookout! Mirrors are everywhere.

Mirrors, Reflections, and Images

In this chapter you will investigate a few of the many places where you can see the images or patterns made by reflecting light. You see an image of your face whenever you look in a mirror. But where does the light needed to make the image come from? Does it come out of your eyes? Or does it come from lightbulbs or sunlight that reflects off your face and body?

Take some time to play with mirrors. Look closely at the images you see in them. Watch what happens to a reflected beam of light when you turn the mirror. Look at the multiple images you sometimes see in a window. Watch your own image change as you move towards or away from a mirror. Where does your image appear to be? How does the brightness of the light affect the images you see in a mirror or window?

1.1   A MIRROR AROUND THE HOUSE

To do this experiment you will need:
- friend to help you
- three small plane (flat) mirrors
- table and chairs
- well-lighted window
- hallway that opens into a room

Hold a small plane mirror in your hand. Look into the mirror. Where does the image of your face appear to be? Can you see the images of other objects around the room? Where do they appear to be? Turn the front (reflecting) side of the mirror toward a well-lighted window. How can you use the mirror to reflect light coming through the window to other parts of the room? Can you see the reflected light on a wall, ceiling, or floor? What happens to the reflected light as you turn the mirror?

Stand at the end of a hallway beside a wall that opens into a room. How can you use the mirror to see objects hidden by the wall?

Finding Your Image in a Mirror

Ask a friend or family member to stand on one side of a wall near a doorway, while you stand on the other side. Because there is a wall between you and the other person, you cannot see each other directly. Hold a mirror in the doorway, as shown in Figure 1. Can you see an image of the person on the other side of the wall? Can he or she see your image?

Have the same person stand beside you in front of a mirror that hangs on a wall. You can see each other's image in the mirror. In fact, you can see both images. Can the other person see both images?

Now move to one side of the mirror so you cannot see your own image. Where does your friend or family member have to stand so you can see his or her image? When you can see his or her image, can he or she see your image? Can the other person see his or

doorway

person on other side of wall

mirror

1) Using a mirror to see someone on the other side of a wall.

her own image? Try looking for one another's image by moving to various places. Is there any place you can stand so that you can see the other person's image but he or she cannot see your image? Is there any place the other person can stand and see your image while you are unable to see his or her image?

Try this same experiment using two mirrors turned so they reflect light in opposite directions, as shown in Figure 2. Sit on one side of a table. Ask a friend to sit on the opposite side of the table. How should you place the two mirrors so that light reflected from both mirrors allows you and your friend to see each other's image? If light reflects from three mirrors, how should they be arranged in order to see each other's image?

Using a single mirror, where can you stand so that you cannot see your image or anyone else's?

PUZZLER 1.1
Why is it that if you can see someone's image in a mirror, that person can see your image as well? Where can you stand so there will be no image of you in a mirror?

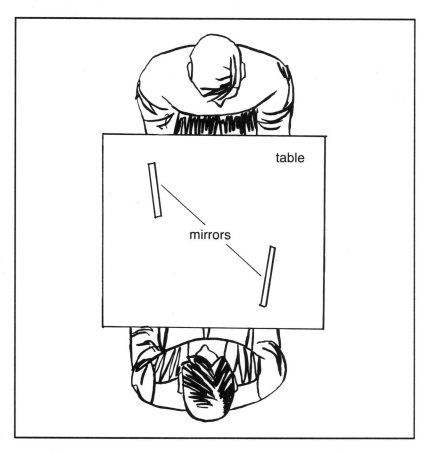

2) Top view of a table and two mirrors. How can the two people arrange the mirrors so they can see each other's images after light is reflected from both mirrors?

1.2   OUTDOOR REFLECTIONS FROM MIRRORS AND GLASS

To do this experiment you will need:
- small plane mirror
- cardboard
- white paper
- glass door that faces the sun
- sunlight
- tape
- modeling clay
- pencil

Take a small mirror outside on a sunny day. *(Caution: Sunlight can permanently damage a person's eyes. Never look directly at the sun and never reflect sunlight into your own or anyone else's eyes.)* Can you use the mirror to reflect a beam of sunlight onto the ground? Onto the side of a building? How should you turn the mirror to make the reflected beam of sunlight move to the right, move to the left, move up, or move down?

Look closely at the area in front of a glass door onto which sunlight is shining. Does the glass reflect sunlight? How can you tell?

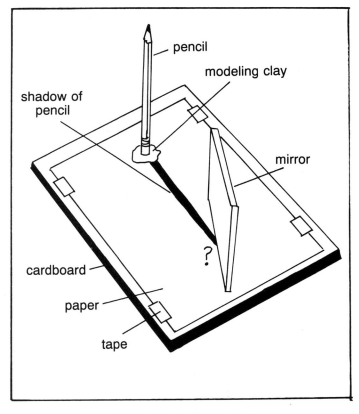

3) Can a shadow be reflected?

If you hold your hand in the sunlight in front of the glass, can you find a shadow of your hand on the ground in front of the glass? If you can, what does this tell you?

To see how a shadow is reflected, place a sheet of cardboard on a level area in bright sunshine in the early morning or late afternoon. Tape a sheet of white paper to the cardboard. Use a small piece of modeling clay to support a pencil upright on the cardboard (see Figure 3). Place a mirror on the pencil's shadow. Is the shadow reflected? How can you tell?

PUZZLER 1.2
A shadow is an area in which light is blocked out. If there is no light in a shadow, how can a shadow be reflected?

SURPRISE 1.1
If possible, use a mirror to reflect sunlight onto a distant building or through an open door or window onto an inside wall. How does the shape of the reflected beam change as it moves farther from the mirror? To see this effect over a shorter distance, use scissors to cut a small square in a piece of paper and tape it over the mirror (see Figure 4). Ask a friend to hold a cardboard screen close to the mirror. Then ask your friend to move the screen farther from the mirror, while keeping the reflected beam on the screen. What happens to the shape of the beam as it moves farther from the mirror. What happens to the size of the reflected beam?

a) Cut a square hole in a piece of paper.

b) Tape

Tape the paper over the reflecting surface of a mirror.

c) Use the small square hole to reflect sunlight. "Capture" the reflected beam on a cardboard screen.

4) Reflecting a small, square beam of light.

(Caution: Sunlight can permanently damage a person's eyes. Never look directly at the sun and never reflect sunlight into your own or anyone else's eyes.)

1.3   IMAGES IN GLASS

To do this experiment you will need:
- window in well-lighted room that you can look through from both inside and outside
- darkness

When it is dark outside, stand in front of a window in a well-lighted room. Can you see your image in the window? What other images can you see in the window glass?

Go outside where it is dark and look into the same room through the same window. Can you see your image when you are on the outside looking in? Why do you think your image is so much brighter on one side of the glass than on the other?

On a bright sunny day, stand outside with the sun at your back and look into the window of a building. Can you see your image in the glass?

Now go to the shady side of the building and look into another window. How does the image you see in the shade compare with the one you saw in bright sunshine? In the late morning or early afternoon, a building casts a rather short shadow. Try to find a window where you can see your image as you stand in shade (in the building's shadow) and in the sun. Is your image brighter when you stand in the sun or in the shade? Can you explain why?

1.4   MULTIPLE IMAGES AND REFLECTIONS IN GLASS

To do this experiment you will need:

- double-paned window or window and storm window in lit room at night
- single window pane in lit room at night
- two mirrors: a front surface mirror, and an ordinary rear surface (silvered) mirror

At night, in a well-lighted room, place your finger on the inside surface of a single-paned window. You will see a bright image of your finger. Look closely! Can you see a second image? Why do you think there are two images? Why is one fainter than the other? If the overlap of the images makes it difficult to distinguish one image from the other, use a pin or a nail instead of your finger. Find a double-paned window—one with two glass panes separated by an air space—or a single-paned window with a storm window behind it. Again, place your finger on the inside pane. Look closely. How many images can you see this time? How can you explain each image?

Front Surface and Rear Surface Mirrors

Now look at two kinds of mirrors (see Chapter 6). A piece of shiny metal is a front surface mirror because light reflects off the metal, which is the outer surface of the mirror. To reach the reflecting surface of a rear surface mirror, light must first pass through the glass in front of the reflecting surface. Most ordinary mirrors are rear surface mirrors (see the beginning of Chapter 6). Rear surface mirrors have a fine layer of silver, which is a good reflector of light, on one side of the glass. Because the smooth side of the silver layer is against the glass, light passes through the glass before being reflected. The other side of the silver, which is on what we call the back of the mirror, is not as smooth. If you look into it you will not see any reflected light.

Place your finger against a front surface mirror or a flat, shiny metal surface. How many images of your finger do you see? Now, place your finger on an ordinary rear surface mirror. Look closely. You can see two images of your finger. One is fainter than the other. Which image seems to touch the outer surface of the glass, the fainter or the brighter one? What does that tell you?

PUZZLER 1.3
Why do you see two images when you hold your finger against a single-paned window? Which is the fainter one? Why do you see four images in a double-paned window? Why is there only one image when you touch a front surface mirror or a shiny metal surface? Why are two images seen in a rear surface mirror? Why is it that now your finger touches the fainter one?

1.5 WHERE IS THE IMAGE SEEN IN A MIRROR?

To do this experiment you will need:
- modeling clay
- mirror
- ruler

Use a piece of modeling clay to support a mirror upright on a table or counter. Place the end of a ruler against the mirror, as shown in Figure 5. Place a small lump of modeling clay at the 3-centimeter or 3-inch line. Look into the mirror. How far behind the mirror does

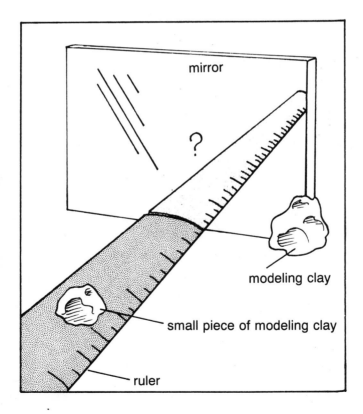

5) Where is the image you see in a mirror?

the modeling clay appear to be? Move the modeling clay to a position farther from the mirror. Where does the image appear to be now? Move the modeling clay closer to the mirror. What happens to the image?

For all the positions you tested, how does the distance from the mirror to the modeling clay's image compare with the distance from the mirror to the real modeling clay?

1.6   MAGIC AND GHOSTS THROUGH IMAGES IN GLASS

To do this experiment you will need:
- adult to help you
- pane of clear, rigid plastic or window glass
- bricks or paperweights
- candleholder
- cookie tin or bread box
- large beaker or jar (quart or liter size is good)
- dark room
- masking tape (if glass is used)
- short candle
- matches
- ruler

This experiment will help you to confirm what you found about the location of mirror images in Experiment 1.5. As you saw, the image of an object appears to be as far behind the mirror as the object is in front of the mirror. If that is true, you should be able to place the image of a candle flame reflected by transparent glass inside a jar of water. People seeing the candle's image in the jar might think they were seeing a candle burning underwater.

19

The "Underwater Candle"

To do this experiment, you will need a pane of clear, rigid plastic or window glass. If you use window glass rather than clear, rigid plastic, **ask an adult** to help you by placing masking tape around the edges of the pane of window glass. The tape will prevent you from being cut by a sharp edge. The adult can then help you arrange bricks or paperweights to support the glass in an upright position (see Figure 6). In a dark room, place a candle in a candleholder. **Ask the adult** to light the candle and place it about 15 centimeters (6 inches) in front of the glass or plastic pane.

Put a large water-filled beaker or jar behind the transparent sheet of glass or plastic. Move the beaker or jar until it looks as though the image of the burning candle is underwater when you look through the glass from behind the candle. If you have the container of water at the same place as the apparent position of the candle's image, the candle will appear to be underwater from any angle you view it through the glass.

Measure the distance from the candle to the glass. Then measure the distance from the glass to the center of the jar. How do these distances compare? What does this tell you about the position of the candle, as compared with the position of its image?

If you move the candle closer to the glass, do you also have to move the jar of water closer to the glass to make the candle's image appear to be underwater? If you move the candle farther from the glass, do you also have to move the jar of water farther from the glass to make the candle's image appear to be underwater?

Move your own face closer to and farther from the glass or plastic. Does your image appear to behave in the same way as the candle's image?

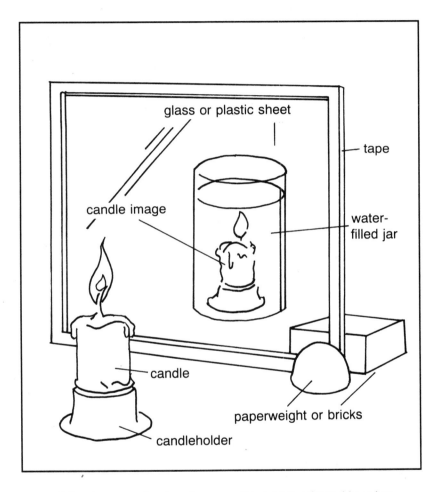

6) The image of a burning candle can be found in a jar of water behind a sheet of glass or plastic.

Put the candle at a convenient distance from the glass and again move the container until the burning candle's image appears to be underwater. Then hide the candle so that only the glass, jar, and image are visible. You can hide the candle with a cookie tin, a metal bread box, or another material that will not burn. You may be able to convince a friend or a family member that you have a magic candle that burns underwater! (**Caution: don't surround a lighted candle with materials that will burn.**)

Seeing Ghosts

A method similar to the "underwater candle" is often used in the theater to produce a ghost on a stage. A sheet of glass is placed at an angle to the audience at the rear of the stage. The actors stand in front of the glass. To one side of the curtain stands an actor dressed as a ghost. A bright light shines on the "ghost," as seen in Figure 7a. The image of the ghost is seen by the audience who are not aware of the clear glass. Use Figure 7b as a guide to set up a model of such a theatrical ghost.

1.7   LIGHT, SIGHT, AND REFLECTIONS

To do this experiment you will need:
- adult to help you
- dark closet or similar dark space
- mirror

In all the experiments you have done so far, light has been present. There is a good reason for this. Without light from the sun or some other source, there can be

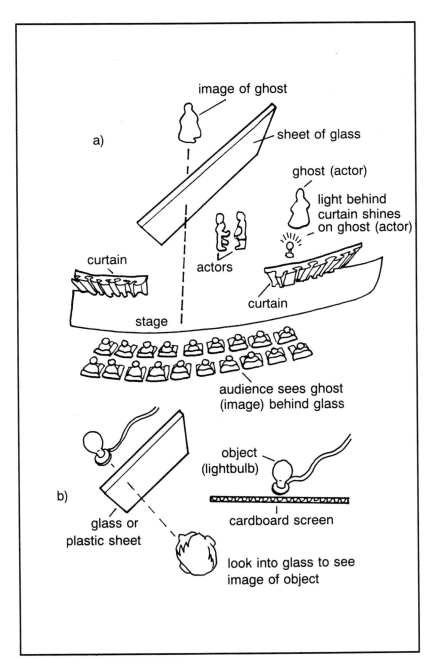

image of ghost

a)

sheet of glass

ghost (actor)

light behind
curtain shines
on ghost (actor)

curtain

actors

curtain

stage

audience sees ghost
(image) behind glass

b)

object
(lightbulb)

cardboard screen

glass or
plastic sheet

look into glass to see
image of object

7a) Making a ghost appear onstage (top view).

b) Model of the way ghosts are made to appear
onstage.

no images or reflections. Despite what you may have read in the comics or seen on television, you do not see by light that comes out of your eyes. Almost every object you see is made visible by light that reflects off the object and goes into your eyes.

To demonstrate that light does not come out of your eyes and that some other source of light is needed to see images, take a mirror into a totally dark closet or similar dark space. **Ask an adult** to help you to be sure that you do not get locked in the dark place. Hold the mirror in front of your face. Can you see any light coming out of your eyes? Can you see any images in the mirror?

Come out of the darkness into a well-lighted space. Can you see images when you look into the mirror now? What evidence do you have that light does not come out of your eyes? What evidence do you have that light is needed to produce images of objects?

1.8   MIRROR WRITING

To do this experiment you will need:
- friend to help you
- small and large mirrors
- modeling clay
- paper and pencil
- clock or watch

Leonardo da Vinci, the Italian artist who painted the "Mona Lisa" and "The Last Supper," was also a brilliant scientist. Unlike modern scientists, he tried to keep his discoveries secret. To do this, he wrote all his notes in such a way that a mirror was needed to read them.

Try writing your name so that it can be read in a mirror. Not easy, is it? Before you try to write like Leonardo did again, look closely at your own image in a mirror. When you wink your right eye, which eye does your image wink? When you raise your left hand, which hand does your image raise? Hold a small clock or a watch upright with its face turned towards the mirror. Can you tell what time it is by looking at the image of the clock's face in the mirror? Watch the clock's second hand. (If it does not have a second hand watch its minute hand for several minutes.) Do the clock hands appear to turn clockwise or counterclockwise?

Reading Signs in a Mirror

Have you ever seen an ambulance with the writing shown in Figure 8? Why do you think it is written in this way on the front of the ambulance?

Have a friend hold Figure 8 behind you while you pretend to be the driver of a car. Hold a mirror as if it were the car's rearview mirror. When you look into the mirror, what does the word in Figure 8 look like to you? Where on Figure 8 should you place a mirror in order to read the word written there?

Try writing some messages to a friend that he or she can read by using a mirror. Do you find that your ability to write such messages improves with practice?

Can you learn to read mirror messages without using a mirror? To find out, try reading the message in Figure 9. Do you think Leonardo used a mirror to read his notes?

Place a mirror on a sheet of white paper so that the reflecting surface of the mirror is facing you. Use a

8) Why are backward letters like these often seen on the front of ambulances?

IF YOU CAN
READ THIS YOU
DON'T NEED A
MIRROR

9) Can you read this message without a mirror?

piece of modeling clay to support the mirror in an upright position. Try to draw a picture of an object while looking into the mirror. Hold your other hand in front of you so you cannot look directly at the drawing.

1.9   MIRRORS AND SYMMETRY

To do this experiment you will need:
- paper and pencil   • small mirror
- front-on facial photograph

Most animals have bilateral symmetry. This means that the right side of their bodies is the same as the left side. Humans are bilaterally symmetrical. Some animals have other symmetries. Starfish and sea urchins, for example, have radial symmetry. They are the same along lines that extend out from a central point.

Some letters of the alphabet have bilateral symmetry. An uppercase (capital) A is the same on both sides of a line drawn through its middle (see Figure 10a). If you place a mirror along the dotted line shown in the drawing, you will see the entire letter A when you look into the mirror. The image of one half of the A joins nicely with the other half on the page. Together they form an A when you place a mirror along the line that divides the letter symmetrically.

Testing Letters and Words for Symmetry

Use your mirror to test the other uppercase letters for symmetry. Which letters have bilateral symmetry?

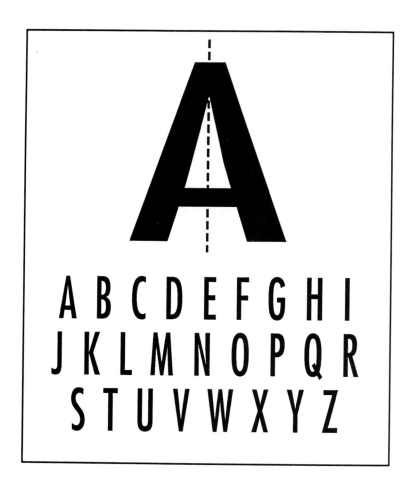

10a) The letter *A* is bilaterally symmetrical. To see the symmetry, place a mirror on the dotted line.

  b) Test these capital letters for symmetry. Which ones are symmetrical?

Prepare your own list of lowercase letters. Which of the lowercase letters are bilaterally symmetrical?

  Can you find words with bilateral symmetry? For example, place a mirror along the dotted line of the word shown in Figure 11. You will find that the upper

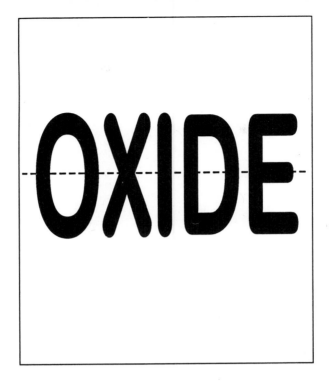

11) Place a mirror on the dotted line. How can you tell that the upper and lower halves of "OXIDE" are symmetrical? What is the meaning of oxide?

and lower halves of the word are symmetrical. What other words have bilateral symmetry? Can you find any in which the right and left sides of the word are symmetrical?

Find a front-on facial photograph of yourself, a family member, or someone you know well. Place a mirror on the picture along the line of symmetry. Look at the picture and the reflected image carefully. Does the face of the person whose photograph you are examining have perfect bilateral symmetry? How can you tell?

1.10   THE LAW OF REFLECTION

To do this experiment you will need:
- friend to help you
- cardboard
- tape—clear and black
- small mirror
- pencil
- ball that bounces well, such as a tennis ball
- large comb
- white paper
- protractor
- modeling clay
- ruler
- sunlight or a dark room with a single bright lightbulb

Drop a ball onto the floor. You will see that it bounces straight back in the direction from which it came. Now roll the ball along a smooth floor so that it hits the wall at an angle, as shown in Figure 12. Try not to give the ball any sideways spin as you roll it. How

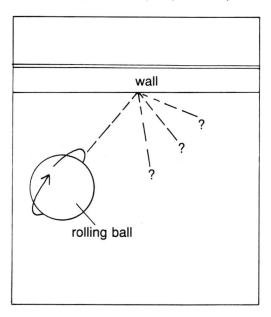

12) How does the angle at which a ball hits a wall compare with the angle at which it reflects off the wall?

does the angle at which the ball reflects (bounces) off the wall compare with the angle at which it hits the wall? Try rolling the ball into the wall at different angles. Each time you roll the ball, watch the angle at which the ball is reflected off the wall. How does the angle at which the ball hits the wall compare with the angle at which it reflects off the wall?

Bouncing Light Beams

If light behaves in the same way as a ball bouncing off a wall, many of the things you have observed in this chapter can be explained. To see if light does behave like a ball bouncing off a wall, observe what happens when a narrow beam of light strikes a mirror. Such a beam is often called a ray of light. Actually, an ideal ray has no width, but for practical purposes you can call a very narrow beam of light a ray.

To see how a beam of ordinary light can be broken up into rays, you will need a large comb, a piece of cardboard with a sheet of white paper taped to it, and a friend to help you. If possible, take the comb and cardboard outside on a sunny day. Turn the cardboard toward the sun (or toward a light bulb on the far side of a dark room). *(Caution: Sunlight can permanently damage a person's eyes. Never look directly at the sun and never reflect sunlight into your own or anyone else's eyes.)* Ask a friend to hold the comb on the end of the paper nearest the sun so that it produces many long narrow beams (rays) of light, as shown in

Figure 13a. Look at the rays closely. Do light rays from the sun appear to be parallel?

Place the mirror on the paper to reflect the rays. Do the reflected rays appear to be parallel?

Use black tape to cover all but one opening near the center of the comb, as shown in Figure 13b. Then fasten the comb to the white paper with a piece of

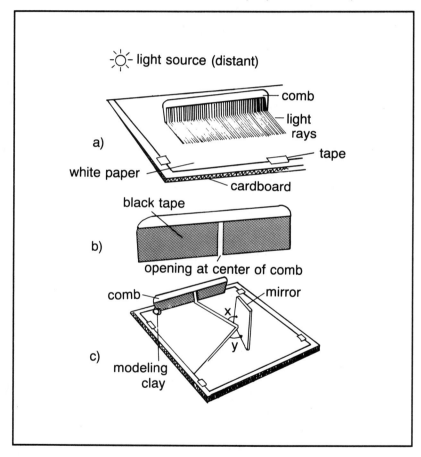

13a) A comb in sunlight will form a number of light rays.

b) Cover all but one opening in the comb with black tape.

c) How do angles x and y compare?

modeling clay. Sunlight or light from a distant lightbulb in an otherwise dark room will form a single ray of light when it passes through the narrow opening. Use a small mirror to reflect the light ray. Turn the mirror and watch what happens when the light strikes the mirror at different angles. For all the different angles you try, how does the angle at which the light ray strikes the mirror (angle x in Figure 13c) compare with the angle at which the reflected ray leaves the mirror (angle y in Figure 13c)? Do they appear to be equal?

Light Ray Angles

You can do an experiment to see if angles x and y are equal. Have a friend hold the mirror in place while you draw a line along the front of it. If your friend should accidentally move the mirror, he or she can always put it back on the line.

Now draw a line along the incoming ray and another along the reflected ray. Remove the mirror and use a ruler to extend all the lines you drew. Use a protractor to measure angles x and y, as shown in Figure 14. Be sure the 0° and 180° marks are on the mirror line. The center of the protractor should be at the point where the incoming and reflected rays meet or (for a rear surface mirror) at a point midway between where these rays cross the mirror line. How does angle x compare with angle y? Are they equal or very nearly so?

Repeat the experiment several times. Each time, make sure the angle at which the light ray strikes the mirror is quite different. What can you conclude about angles x and y in every test you made?

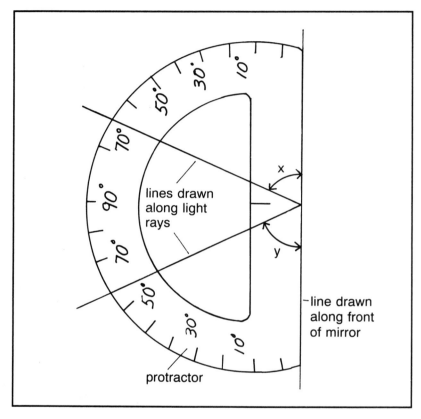

14) Measuring angles with a protractor.

Science Principle: Law of Reflection

In Experiment 1.10, you probably found that the angle at which a ray of light strikes a mirror is equal to the angle at which it is reflected from the mirror. This is known as the Law of Reflection. If you think about it, the Law of Reflection of light can explain all that you have observed about mirrors.

1.11   RAYS AND IMAGES

To do this experiment you will need:
- friend to help you
- black tape
- white paper
- small mirror
- sunlight or a dark room
  with a single bright lightbulb
- large comb
- cardboard
- protractor
- modeling clay
- pencil
- ruler

You may wonder how the Law of Reflection can explain the images you have seen reflected in mirrors. To see how images are formed in a plane mirror, use black tape to cover all but two of the spaces between the teeth of the large comb, as shown in Figure 15. The two spaces should be about 1 centimeter (3/8 inch)

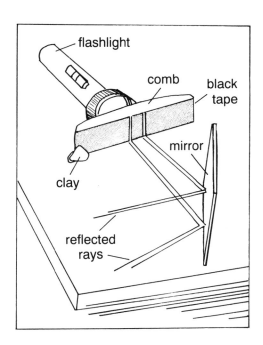

15) Reflected rays form the images you see in mirrors.

apart. Use modeling clay to support the comb on a sheet of white paper taped to cardboard, as you did in Experiment 1.10. Shine the light from a small flashlight through the comb to make two diverging rays (rays that spread apart). Place a mirror on the rays. You will see that the two rays reflect from the mirror and continue to spread apart. For each ray, the law of reflection holds true. Where do the reflected rays appear to be coming from? Together, all the rays from an object that are reflected by a mirror give rise to an image.

PUZZLER 1.4
How does the Law of Reflection explain the formation of images in plane mirrors?

PUZZLER 1.5
Smooth glass, metal, or plastic reflects light and forms clear images. Why can't you see images by looking at a smooth white file card?

One-way mirrors, which are partially silvered, allow people outside a brightly lighted room to look in without being seen by those inside the room. A partially silvered mirror allows some light to pass through the glass, while reflecting the rest. Much of the light from a brightly lighted room will pass through partially silvered glass walls making the inside visible to people in a dimly lighted area outside the room. Enough light is reflected back so that people within the room think they are looking into a mirror and are unaware of any outside observers.

Other Mirrors and Their Reflections

Not all mirrors are flat. If you look closely at the mirror on the right-hand side of most cars, you will find that its reflecting surface is curved. It bulges slightly outward. The same is true of some of the mirrors found on trucks or the mirrors used in stores to detect shoplifters. They, too, have an outward (*convex*) curvature. On the other hand, the mirrors found in telescopes or makeup and shaving mirrors curve inward. They have a saucer-shaped (*concave*) reflecting surface.

Science Principle: The Law of Reflection for Mirrors

The Law of Reflection holds true whether a mirror is flat or curved. Careful measurements of the angles between incoming (incident) and reflected light rays show that the angle between an incoming ray and the mirror is the same as the angle between the reflected ray and the mirror (see Figure 16a). Because this law holds true for all reflecting surfaces, light striking convex mirrors is spread apart (diverges); light striking concave mirrors comes together (converges). See the drawings in Figure 16b and 16c.

2.1 IMAGES IN SPOONS

To do this experiment you will need:
• various sizes of bright, shiny spoons

Look into a bright, shiny soupspoon. Look into the side that holds the soup. It is the concave side of the spoon. You will see an upside-down image of yourself. What happens to the size of your image as you move the spoon closer to your face? What happens to the size of your image as you move the spoon farther from your face? Place the spoon very close to your eye. Can you see a very large image of your eye?

Can you see images of other objects in the spoon?

Turn the spoon over so that you look into its convex side. How do these images compare with the ones you saw in the concave surface? If you hold the convex side close to your eye, do you see a magnified image of your eye, or is it about the size of your real eye?

Repeat the experiment with a larger spoon, such as a serving spoon. Generally, a larger spoon has less curvature—it is not as convex or concave as a smaller spoon. Hold the large spoon and the small spoon side

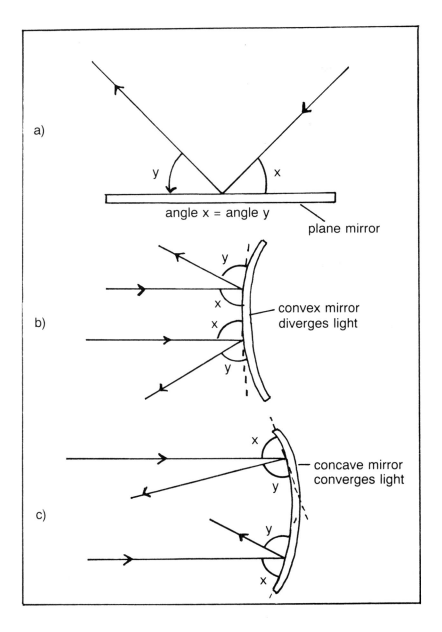

a)

angle x = angle y

plane mirror

b)

convex mirror diverges light

c)

concave mirror converges light

16) Angles x and y are equal for all reflecting surfaces.

by side. In which spoon are the images larger? Is this true on both the convex and concave sides of the spoons?

Teaspoons are generally longer and narrower than soupspoons. What do the images you see in the spoon look like when you hold the spoon as shown in Figure 17a? What do the images you see look like when you hold the spoon as shown in Figure 17b? Are images in both the convex and concave sides affected in the same way?

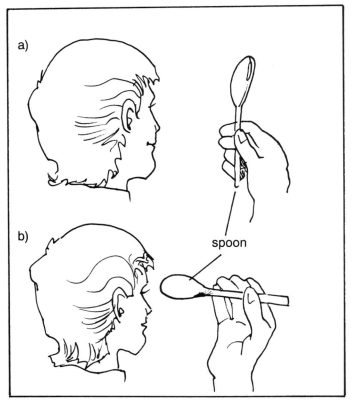

a)

b)

spoon

17) How does the way you hold the spoon affect the image you see?

2.2   CURVED MIRRORS

To do this experiment you will need:
- facial tissue
- convex mirror, such as a right-hand side-view mirror in a car or truck, or a pair of sunglasses
- shiny soupspoon
- concave mirror, such as a shaving or makeup mirror

Concave Mirrors

Find a mirror with a concave surface such as a makeup or shaving mirror. Cover your fingertips with a facial tissue and feel the surface of the mirror. Your fingertips will tell you that the surface is concave, but much less curved than a soupspoon. Now hold the mirror close to your face and look into it. What do you notice about the image you see? How does the image compare with the one you saw in a concave soupspoon? Slowly move away from the mirror. With each step, be sure you can still see your image in the mirror. You will reach a point where your image becomes inverted (upside down). Is this image similar to the one you saw in a soupspoon?

Convex Mirrors

Now look into a convex mirror. If you cannot find a convex mirror, use a pair of sunglasses. The front surfaces of the sunglasses are convex—they curve outward. Place the glasses or the mirror on a table in a well-lighted room. Look into the mirror or into the front surface of one lens of the sunglasses. Notice that you can see your image and the images of a number of nearby objects. How does the size of these images compare with the ones you can see in a plane (flat) mirror?

To find out, place a small plane mirror beside the glasses. How do the sizes of images seen in the convex mirror compare with the sizes of the same images seen in a plane mirror? Are both sets of images right-side up or upside down?

How do the images you see in a convex mirror compare with the ones you saw in the convex side of a soupspoon? Which is more curved, the soupspoon or the mirror?

PUZZLER 2.1
How does the curvature of a convex mirror affect the size of the images seen in the mirror?

2.3 WHICH IMAGES CAN BE "CAPTURED"?

To do this experiment you will need:
- adult to help you
- white paper
- convex mirror
- slide projector and slide
- cardboard (about 30 centimeters or 1 square foot)
- tape
- concave mirror
- plane mirror
- yardstick

Make a screen by taping a sheet of white paper to a piece of cardboard. Find a room with a bright window. Have a friend stand on the side of the room opposite the window. He or she can hold a concave mirror with its reflecting surface turned toward the window. Hold the cardboard screen in front of the mirror so that reflected light falls on the screen. Move the cardboard until you see on the screen clear images of the objects seen through the window. You have "captured" a real image on the screen. Real images are images that can be seen on a screen. Images that can be seen in a mirror but cannot be captured on a screen are called "virtual images."

Try capturing images on a screen using a convex mirror. Are the images formed by a convex mirror real or virtual?

Try capturing images on a screen using a plane mirror. Are the images formed by a plane mirror real or virtual?

The images made with a slide projector are real images too. The lens at the front of a slide projector bends light coming through the slide to form the image you see on a screen.

PUZZLER 2.2
Why can a concave mirror form real images but convex and plane mirrors form only virtual images?

Ask an adult to help you place a slide in a slide projector and capture a clear image of the slide on the screen you used earlier. Hold a yardstick above the screen. Remove the screen. At the place where the screen had been located, move the stick rapidly up and down. What do you see?

2.4   CURVED MYLAR MIRRORS

To do this experiment you will need:

- two friends to help you
- flexible cardboard
- flexible reflective Mylar, if available; if not, use reflective Mylar sheets (buy from a paper goods, art supply, or hardware store) or metallic gift-wrapping paper
- scissors
- clear plastic tape
- cylindrical clear glass tumblers or clear plastic soda bottles of different sizes

If you can find flexible Mylar, which is a plastic with a reflective Mylar-coated surface, use it for this experiment. It can easily be bent into a convex or concave surface.

A Convex Mylar Mirror

If you cannot find flexible Mylar, use scissors to cut a piece of flexible cardboard about 15 centimeters (6 inches) on a side. Then cut a piece of Mylar 3 to 5 centimeters (1 to 2 inches) shorter than the cardboard. Have two friends help you tape the Mylar to the cardboard. By holding all corners of the Mylar, your friends can keep it stretched while you tape its edges to the cardboard. Keeping the Mylar stretched will allow you to see your image and be certain that you are making a good plane mirror. (If you can not find Mylar, use metallic gift-wrapping paper. It is not as reflective, but it will do.)

Turn the edges of the cardboard away from you to form a two dimensional convex surface (see Figure 18a). What happens to your image? Does it get shorter or thinner? What happens to your image if you make the Mylar mirror more convex? What happens if you make the mirror less convex?

Turn the mirror 90°, as shown in Figure 18b. What

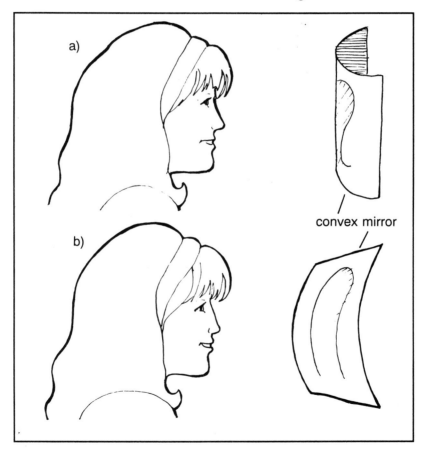

convex mirror

18) What does your image look like in a cylinder-shaped convex mirror?

happens to your image now? Does it get shorter or thinner? What happens as you make the mirror more convex? What happens as you make the mirror less convex?

A *Concave* Mylar Mirror

Unless you have flexible Mylar, it is not as easy to make a concave Mylar mirror. The Mylar will crinkle if you try to flex the cardboard covered with Mylar into a concave shape. To make concave cylindrical mirrors using Mylar sheets or metallic wrapping paper, you can use cylindrical clear glass tumblers or clear plastic soda bottles of different sizes. If you use glass tumblers, simply hold a rectangular sheet of Mylar against the outside wall of the tumbler. Then look through the opposite side of the tumbler into the reflective surface, as shown in Figure 19a.

If you use plastic soda bottles, use scissors to cut away part of the bottle leaving a clear cylindrical wall, as shown in Figure 19b. Again, you can simply hold the Mylar sheet against the outside wall of the bottle and look into the concave side. Incidentally, plastic soda bottles that are round at the bottom and set in sturdy black bases produce very sharp, clear, inverted images. If you look closely, you will see that the area around the bottoms of these bottles acts like a concave mirror.

Whichever material you use, you may have to try different lighting conditions until you see the images clearly because there will be other reflections. Does your image become shorter or thinner?

If you turn this concave mirror 90°, what happens to your image? Does it get shorter or thinner?

You cannot make the glass or plastic more or less

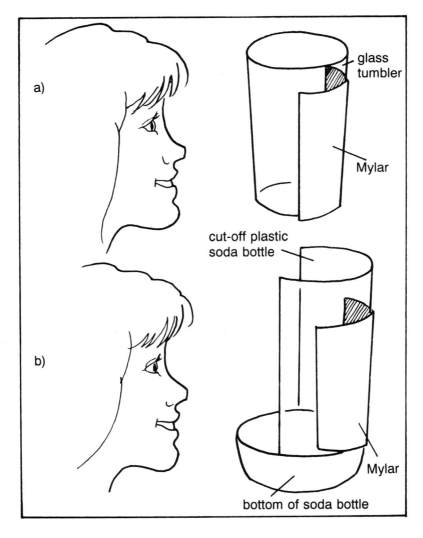

19) Making cylinder-shaped concave mirrors using Mylar and: a) glass tumblers, or b) cut-off plastic soda bottles.

concave, but you can use a larger or a smaller glass or plastic bottle. This will change the curvature of your Mylar mirror. What happens to your image as you make the mirror more concave? What happens as you make the mirror less concave?

2.5   A ONE-WAY MIRROR

To do this experiment you will need:
- adult to help you
- sharp knife
- sheets of reflective Mylar (buy from a paper goods, art supply, or hardware store)
- rigid cardboard
- scissors
- clear plastic tape

Find a sheet of rigid cardboard about 1 meter (3 feet) long and 60 centimeters (2 feet) wide. **Ask an adult** to cut an opening in the cardboard. The opening should be about 10 centimeters (4 inches) less on each side than a sheet of Mylar. Then **ask the adult** to help you tape the Mylar over the opening in the cardboard. The Mylar should be smooth and taut. You now have a one-way mirror.

Hold the mirror in front of your face, and turn toward an unlighted wall. Can you see your image in the mirror? Now turn toward a bright window. Can you see the window? What has happened to the brightness of *your* image?

Turn the mirror towards a bright light. Can you see the light through the mirror? How bright is your own image?

Hang a second sheet of Mylar over the first one. How does the second sheet affect your ability to see through the mirror? How does it affect your ability to see images of objects on your side of the mirror?

You might like to build a small room with cardboard walls in one corner of a larger room. The small room should contain lights and a few chairs so people can sit comfortably in the room. What kind of lighting conditions are needed if you want to remain invisible while observing people inside the room? What kind of lighting conditions are needed in the cardboard room if you want people inside the room to remain invisible while they observe people outside the room?

2.6 FUNNY IMAGES IN FUN HOUSE MIRRORS

To do this experiment you will need:
- flexible Mylar or sheets of reflective Mylar (buy from a paper goods, art supply, or hardware store)
- flexible cardboard
- clear plastic tape

If you have the opportunity, visit a fun house and look at your image in some of the mirrors you find there. Can you explain how the mirrors produce the images you see there?

From what you have learned about curved mirrors and mylar, you can make some fun house mirrors of your own. Use flexible Mylar or Mylar sheets taped to flexible cardboard to construct a mirror that will make people look fatter than they really are. Build a mirror that will make people look thinner than they really are. Construct a mirror that will make people appear to be crooked.

2.7 REFLECTIONS FROM A LENS

To do this experiment you will need:
- adult to help you
- magnifying glass (convex lens)
- candle and candleholder
- light-colored wall
- small sheet of white cardboard

Ask an adult to light a candle in a dark room and place it about 1 meter (3 feet) from a light-colored wall. Hold a magnifying glass (a convex lens) between the candle and the wall. Move the lens back and forth. You will find that you can capture a real image of the candle on the wall. This image is made by the lens, which bends (refracts) light that passes through it. The refracted light forms an upside-down image of the candle flame, as shown in Figure 20a.

Now look into the lens from the other side of the flame, as shown in Figure 20b. This allows you to see any images formed by light reflected from the glass lens. How many images do you see? Are any of them upside down?

With the lens between the candle and your eye (see Figure 20c), can you capture any of these images on a screen? To find out, *ask an adult* to hold a small white cardboard screen near the candle while you move and turn the lens to see if you can capture a real image of the candle flame on the screen.

PUZZLER 2.3
Why can you see two images reflected by a convex lens? Why are you able to capture only one of them on a screen?

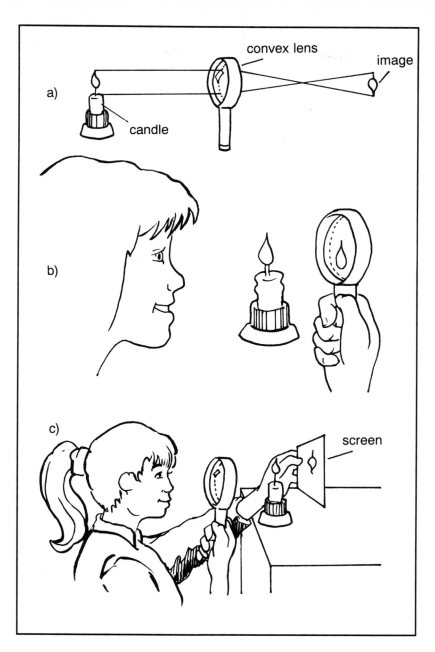

20a) Image formed by refraction of light by lens.

b) Can you see images reflected by lens' surfaces?

c) Can you "capture" reflected images on a screen?

More than 2,000 years ago, Egyptians, Greeks, and Romans made mirrors by polishing metals until they were very smooth.

Multiple Reflections

There are many examples of multiple reflections in nature. Two of the most beautiful are the setting sun and the rising full moon seen on an ocean's horizon. The portion of each wave that makes the proper angle between sun or moon and observer reflects light to your eyes. This produces a band of light that stretches along the sea. Perhaps you have been in a room that has many mirrors. If you have, you saw many images of yourself at the same time. You were probably not surprised to see many images when there were many mirrors. After all, each mirror can reflect light and produce an image from the reflected light. But suppose there are only two mirrors. Can you obtain more than two images?

3.1 TWO MIRRORS AT DIFFERENT ANGLES

To do this experiment you will need:
- 2 large hand mirrors
- table
- clock or watch
- 2 rectangular mirrors
- paper
- colored pen or crayon

Use two hand mirrors, as shown in Figure 21a. Use the first mirror to reflect light coming from objects in front of you onto the second mirror and from there to your eye. View the objects ahead of you by looking into the second mirror, just as you would if you were looking into a periscope. Are the images you see right side up or upside down? Use the same two hand mirrors so that you can see whatever is behind you (see Figure 21b). Again, view the objects by looking at their images in the second mirror. What do you notice about the images of the objects behind you?

> **SURPRISE 3.1**
> Why are the images of the objects behind you upside down when seen by double reflection?

Fusing Two Images into One

Place one rectangular mirror flat on a table. Place a second mirror perpendicular to the first one, as shown in Figure 22a. From what you saw earlier in this experiment, perhaps you can predict what your image will be like if you look into the region where the two mirrors join. Try it! Does your image look the way you predicted it

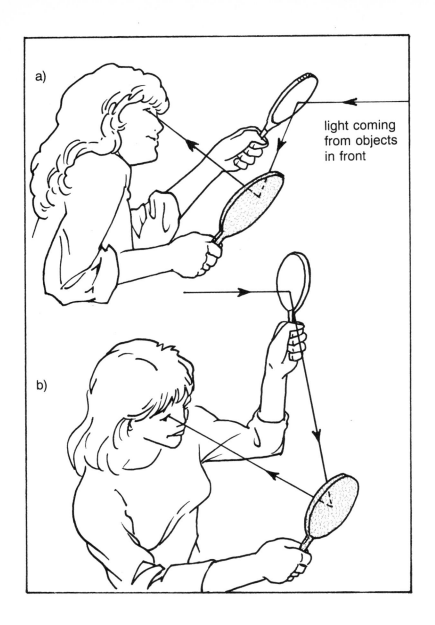

light coming
from objects
in front

21a) Double reflection of light from objects in front of you.

b) Double reflection of light from objects behind you.

would? (You may have to turn the mirror slightly if your image appears to be separated. When your images fuse into one, you can be sure the mirrors are at right angles to one another.) When you wink your right eye, which eye does your image wink?

You can also see images of yourself by looking into each of the two mirrors separately. What do these images look like? Are they ordinary mirror images? How can you tell?

Now place both mirrors perpendicular to the table and to each other, as shown in Figure 22b. Again, look

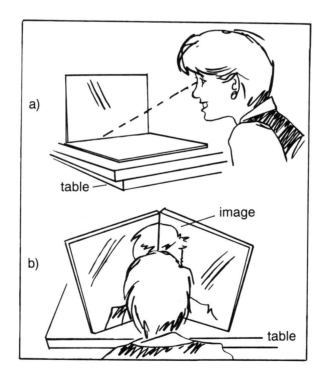

22a) Look into the region where two mirrors perpendicular to one another join.

b) Look into the same two mirrors rotated 90°.

into the region where the two mirrors join. If necessary, adjust the mirrors slightly until your images fuse into one. Look closely at this image. When you wink your right eye, which eye does your image wink? Hold a small clock or a watch upright with its face turned toward the place where the two mirrors join. Can you tell what time it is by looking at the image of the clock's face in the mirror? Watch the clock's second hand. (If it does not have a second hand, watch its minute hand for several minutes.) Do the clock hands appear to turn clockwise or counterclockwise?

You can also see images of yourself and the clock by looking into each of the two mirrors separately. What do these images look like? How can you tell that they are ordinary mirror images?

PUZZLER 3.1
Why is the image of your face upside down when you look into the union of the two mirrors in Figure 22a? When you look into the union of the two mirrors in both Figures 22a and 22b and wink your right eye, your image also winks its right eye. Why?

On a sheet of white paper, make a drawing, such as the one in Figure 23a. Place two rectangular mirrors upright and at right angles to each other in front of the drawing. If you have the two mirrors at an angle of 90°, you will see three images in the mirrors. Which image is the result of two reflections?

Gradually decrease the angle between the mirrors,

as shown in Figure 23b. What happens to the number of images as the angle decreases? How can you tell which images are images of images? What happens if you make the angle between the mirrors greater than a straight angle (greater than 180°), as shown in Figure 23c? Can you explain what you observe?

To see what happens when the angle between the mirrors becomes 0° try Experiment 3.2.

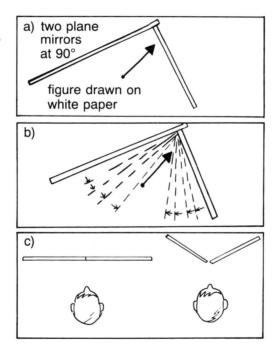

23a) Top view of two mirrors at right angles with a figure between them. How many images of the figure can be seen in the mirrors?

 b) As the angle between the mirrors is made smaller, what happens to the number of images?

 c) If the angle is made greater than a straight angle (180°), what happens to the image?

3.2   TWO PARALLEL MIRRORS

To do this experiment you will need:
- large mirror, such as a bathroom mirror
- large hand mirror

As you know from earlier experiments, it is possible for the same light to be reflected many times. Suppose you want to look at the back of your head. You can do so by standing with your back to a large mirror while looking into a second mirror held in front of you, as shown in Figure 24. Try it! You will be able to see yourself

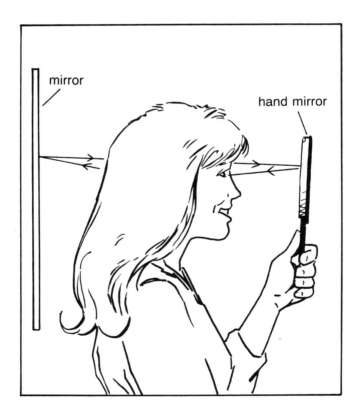

24) A way to see the back of your head.

as someone standing behind you sees you. Light reflected from the back of your head travels to the mirror held behind you. It then reflects off that mirror and travels to the mirror in front of you where it is reflected to your eye.

What do you think you would see if you stood in a hallway that had mirrors on both sides? You can find the answer to this question by standing in front of a large vertical mirror such as a bathroom or full-length mirror. Hold a large hand mirror just below your eyes. The reflecting surface of the hand mirror should be turned toward the large mirror. Try to keep the surfaces of the two mirrors parallel. Can you see your image? Can you see the image of your image? How about the image of the image of your image? How many images can you see? What happens to the sizes of and the distances to the images you see?

PUZZLER 3.2
How can you explain the many images you see in two parallel mirrors?

3.3   THREE MIRRORS

To do this experiment you will need:
- 3 mirrors—identical if possible
- tape
- colored pen or crayon

Place 3 mirrors together, as shown in Figure 25. Use tape to hold them in place. Use a colored pen or crayon to draw on a sheet of white paper the small arrow shown in Figure 23. Place the 3 mirrors on the paper so that they surround the design. Place your eye close to the top of the mirrors and look at the images of the design that you can see in the mirrors. How many images can you see? Can you see more if you look closely? Which images are images of images? How can you tell?

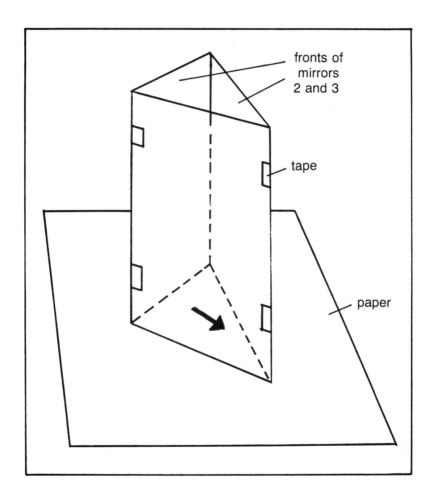

25) Three mirrors surround the figure of a small arrow on a sheet of paper. How many images can you see?

3.4   A KALEIDOSCOPE

To do this experiment you will need:
- small, brightly colored pieces of plastic
- 3 identical mirrors—if possible, use long narrow mirrors, or make your own using cardboard, ruler, Mylar or aluminum foil, glue, knife, and adult to help you
- plastic wrap
- paper tape

Commercial kaleidoscopes consist of three mirrors held together to make a triangular tube. Looking into one end, you see a pattern of colored pieces of glass or plastic at the other end. Rotating the tube causes the pattern to change. If possible, look into such a kaleidoscope and enjoy watching the colored patterns change as you turn the tube.

You can make a simple kaleidoscope of your own by taping three mirrors together, as shown in Figure 26a. Hold one end of the tube near a colored flower. Look through the other end and rotate the tube. Place a colored picture or photograph near one end of the tube. Look through the other end of the tube and rotate the picture. Based on what you saw in the previous experiments, how can you explain what you see in your homemade kaleidoscope?

Making a Kaleidoscope

If you cannot find 3 identical mirrors, you can make a kaleidoscope using cardboard, Mylar or aluminum foil, glue, and a knife, as shown in Figure 26b. **Ask an adult** to use the knife to score the cardboard and cut the

Mylar or aluminum foil to fit three of the rectangles. The three shiny strips can then be glued to the cardboard before it is folded into a triangular tube.

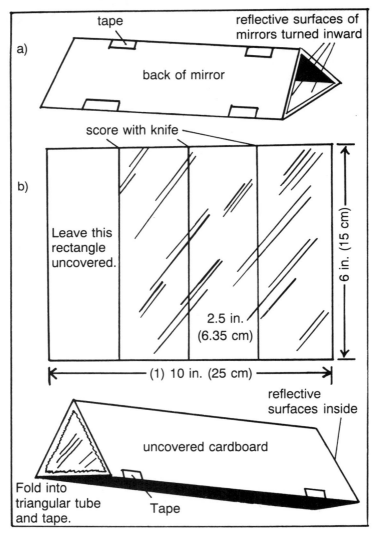

26a) A kaleidoscope made by taping three mirrors together.

b) A kaleidoscope made from cardboard, Mylar, glue, and tape.

3.5　DOUBLE REFLECTION
IN A PRISM

To do this experiment you will need:
- pen or pencil
- 45–45–90 prism (buy from an art supply store or a science supply house, or borrow one from your school)
- white paper
- mirror

As you will find in Chapter 4, Sir Isaac Newton used a prism to reflect light inside his telescope. To see how a prism can be used to reflect light, draw the letter *L* on a piece of paper. Place a plane mirror on the paper above the top of the letter, as shown in Figure 27a. How does the image of the letter seen in the mirror compare with the letter on the paper? Is it reversed? Is it upside down?

The Letter L Through a Prism

Next, place the 45–45–90 prism on the letter, as shown in Figure 27b. Look down through the longest flat surface of the prism to see the *L* through the short-side surface of the prism that is on the letter. Then look into the other short-side surface of the prism to find an image of the *L*. How does it compare with the one you saw in the plane mirror?

Now, place the mirror upright beside the *L*, as shown in Figure 27c. How does the image of the letter seen in the mirror compare with the letter on the paper? Is it reversed? Is it upside down? Place the 45–45–90 prism on the *L*, as shown in Figure 27d. Look down through the

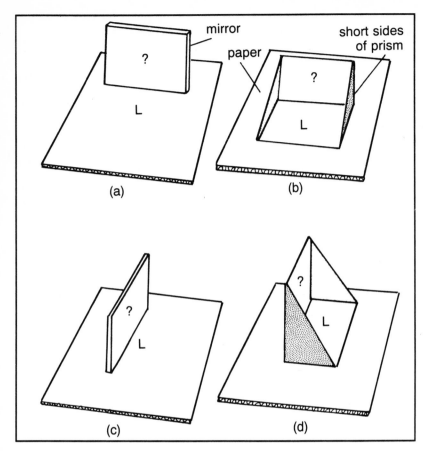

(a)   (b)

(c)   (d)

27a) A mirror is placed perpendicular to the letter L on a sheet of paper. What does the image of the L look like in the mirror?

b) The short-side surface of a 45-45-90 prism is placed on the L. Look through the long-side surface of the prism. What does the image of the L look like in the other short-side surface of the prism?

c) The mirror is now placed to one side of the L. What does the image of the L look like?

d) The prism in b) is turned 90°. Again, look through the long-side surface of the prism. What does the image of the L look like in the other short-side surface of the prism?

longest flat surface of the prism to see the L through the short-side surface of the prism that is over the letter. Then look into the other short-side surface of the prism. Can you see an image of the L? How does it compare with the one you saw in the plane mirror?

Based on what you have seen in this experiment, why was Newton able to use a prism to replace a mirror in his telescope?

SURPRISE 3.2
Look into the prism, as set up in Figure 27b, to view the letter through the longest surface of the prism. Gradually, lower your head so as to view the letter at a larger angle. Why does the letter disappear?

3.6   TOTAL INTERNAL REFLECTION

To do this experiment you will need:
- 45–45–90 prism
- scissors
- bright light
- sheet of white cardboard
- black construction paper
- dark room

In Surprise 3.2, you saw that the letter L disappeared when you viewed it from a large angle. To see why the L and its image disappeared, you will need a narrow beam of light and the prism you used in the previous experiment.

Place the prism on a sheet of white cardboard. Use scissors to cut a rectangle about 15 centimeters (6 inches) long and 10 centimeters (4 inches) high from a piece of black construction paper. At the center of the long side, use the scissors to cut a narrow slit about 1 millimeter (1/16 inch) wide. Fold each end of the rectangle so it will stand by itself and place it on the cardboard in front of the prism, as shown in Figure 28a. Let light from a single distant lightbulb in an otherwise dark room shine through the slit in the black rectangle to make a narrow beam of light.

Light Reflected by a Prism

Place the prism on the light beam so that the beam is perpendicular to the long surface of the prism, as shown in Figure 28a. This will cause the beam to strike the short-side surface at an angle of 45°. Notice that none of the light in this beam goes out through the short side. All the light is reflected to the other short side of the prism and back out through the long surface of the prism. As a result, the light goes back in the opposite direction to that from which it entered the prism.

The fact that all the light inside glass is reflected when it strikes a glass-to-air surface at 45° is called total internal reflection. In fact, all light striking such a surface at an angle greater than 42° will be reflected inside the glass. None of the light will pass through the surface into the air.

Breaking Light into Colors

If you turn the prism slightly, as shown in Figure 28b, to make the angle a little less than 42° (the so-called critical angle) some of the light will come out through the short side of the prism into the air. This beam almost touches the outside surface of the prism. Notice that the refracted beam is colored. In fact, it contains all the colors in the rainbow.

Look at the beam very closely. If necessary, examine the beam with a magnifying glass. Which color of light is refracted the most? Which color is refracted the least?

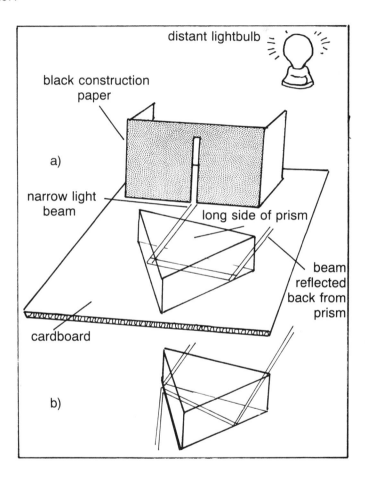

28a) A narrow beam of light perpendicular to the long surface of the prism is reflected back in the opposite direction. No light emerges through the short-side surface of the prism.

b) If the angle at which the light strikes the short-side surface of the prism is less than 42°, some light will emerge into the air.

Brighter light, such as sunlight, will produce more intense colors. If possible, take a prism outdoors. Hold the prism in a beam of sunlight and turn it in front of a white surface until you see a rainbow of color. *(Caution: Sunlight can permanently damage a person's eyes. Never look directly at the sun and never reflect sunlight into your own or anyone else's eyes.)*

3.7   LIGHT GUIDES

To do this experiment you will need:
- friend to help you
- hammer and nail
- sink
- bright flashlight
- mirror
- tall clear glass tumbler
- optical fiber light guide or optical fibers and black plastic tape (buy from a hobby store or a science supply house or borrow one from your school)
- water
- dark paper
- dark room
- board or block
- penny (or other coin)
- coffee can
- large clear jar with screw-on lid
- aluminum pan at least 7.5 centimeters (3 inches) deep

You can buy an optical fiber light guide in a hobby store, from a science supply house, or you might borrow one from your school. Or, you can make your own light guide by wrapping a 30 centimeter (1 foot) long bundle of optical fibers with black plastic tape.

To see how your light guide uses total internal reflection to transmit light, look into one end of the guide while you cover the other end with your finger. Hold the end covered by your finger close to a window or another source of light. Now remove your finger. How can you tell that light is transmitted along the optical fibers? Bend the light guide into various shapes. Does light still follow the fibers when the guide is bent?

Water as a Light Guide

Even water can be used as a light guide. Light moving from water into air will also be totally reflected if the light strikes the surface at an angle greater than 48°.

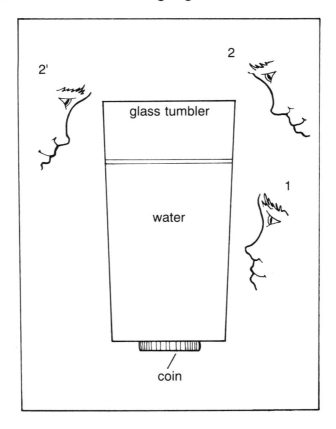

29) The coin under the glass is visible when the glass is empty and your eye is at position 1. The coin disappears when water is added to the glass, but at position 2 or 2' an image of the coin can be seen.

To see that light is totally reflected as it passes from water to air at a large enough angle, place a tall clear glass tumbler on a penny (or other coin). Look at the penny through the side of the glass (from position 1), as shown in Figure 29. Have a friend pour water into the glass. You will find that the coin disappears. However, if you look through the water's surface from position 2 or 2', you will see an image of the coin.

PUZZLER 3.3

Why does the coin disappear as water is added to the glass tumbler? Why is an image of the coin visible when your eye is at position 2 or 2'?

Here's another way to see total internal reflection when light passes from air into water. Place a coin on the bottom of an aluminum pan that is at least 7.5 centimeters (3 inches) deep. Fill the pan with water. Place a mirror in the water at an angle to the bottom as shown in Figure 30a. You will be able to see one image of the coin by looking into the mirror at the angle you would expect to see light from the coin reflected by the mirror (position 1 in Figure 30a). But you can also see another image of the coin by looking more directly into the mirror (see position 2). This image must be formed by light that was first reflected by the water's surface.

An even stranger image formed by total internal reflection can be seen with this same water-filled pan and mirror. Place the mirror on the bottom of the pan, as shown by the dotted-line mirror in Figure 30b. Stick your finger into the water above the mirror. You can see the image of your finger that you would expect to see. But now place the mirror at an angle, as you did with the coin (see Figure 30b). Again, stick your finger into the water, as you did before. Look into the mirror from various points until you see the images shown at the right of Figure 30b.

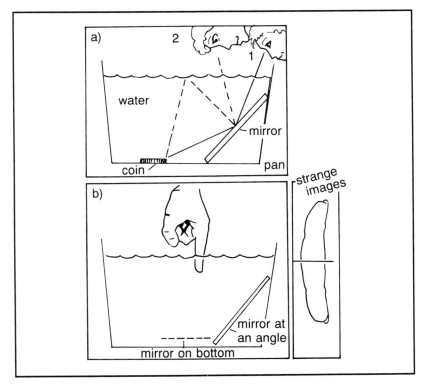

30a) Place your eye at position 1. You will see the image of the coin as expected. Place your eye at position 2. There you can see the image of the coin produced by light from the coin that is totally reflected by the water surface back to the mirror and from there to your eye. The rays for this image are shown as dotted lines.

b) Place your finger in the water as shown. You should be able to see an image like the one seen on the right side of the drawing.

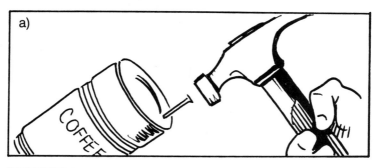

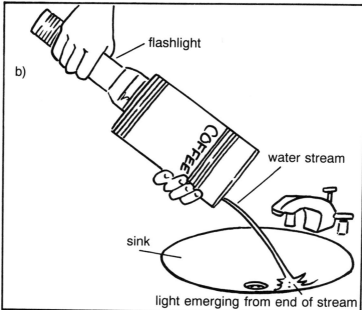

31a) Punch a small hole near the edge of the bottom of an empty coffee can.

b) Hold the can as shown near a bathroom sink. Shine light into the open end of the can. On the sink's surface, you will see light reflected as it emerges from the end of the water stream. The stream of water serves as a light guide.

To make a simple water light guide, use a hammer and nail to punch a small hole near one side of the bottom of a coffee can (see Figure 31a). Place your finger over the hole and half fill the can with water in a dark bathroom. Tip the can, as shown in Figure 31b, so that a stream of water flows into the bathroom sink. At the same time, have a friend shine a flashlight into the open end of the can. You will see light reflected where the stream strikes the bottom or side of the sink. This reflected light traveled along the water stream that flows from the can.

Craftsmen in Venice were probably the first to make glass mirrors. They poured mercury onto a sheet of tinfoil. The mercury was then covered with paper and a sheet of glass was carefully placed on the paper. When the paper was withdrawn, the mercury and tin adhered to the glass to produce a very smooth reflecting surface.

Colored Reflections

Most of the light reflected to your eyes is colored, but some colored reflections and images are more notice-able and spectacular than others. Few things are more beautiful than a brilliant sunset or an awe-inspiring rain-bow that sometimes follows a summer shower. Colored images that arise from our own actions can be seen in a falling soap bubble or one carried gently upward by a light wind. And we may take delight in watching the colors reflected from the ceiling above a Christmas tree or even the colored light reflected from a wet oil slick on a pavement. Colored reflections and images add beauty and interest to our lives.

4.1   A RAINBOW IN YOUR YARD

To do this experiment you will need:
- sunlight
- garden hose

You have probably seen a rainbow in the sky, but you may not know that you can make a small rainbow in your own yard. All it takes is some bright sunlight and a garden hose.

A natural rainbow occurs when raindrops in one part of the sky reflect sunlight from another part of the sky to your eyes. Figure 32 is a simplified drawing showing how the light is bent (refracted) as it enters and leaves a raindrop and how it is reflected from the rear surface of the

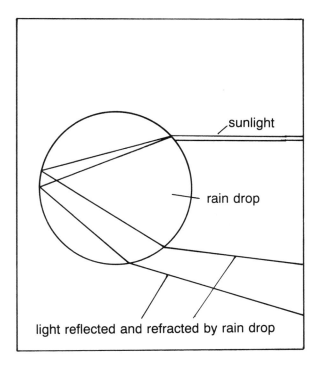

32) Rainbows are seen when sunlight is reflected and refracted by raindrops.

raindrop. Because different colors of light are bent differently when they enter or leave water, the colors that emerge from the raindrops are separated into a spectrum (a range of colors extending from red to violet).

To make a rainbow in your yard, stand with your back to the sun. Use a garden hose to spray a fine mist into the air. Bend and move your head to the side until you can see a rainbow. Where else do you sometimes see small rainbows like the one you can see with the garden hose? Where else do you sometimes see rainbowlike colors in the sky?

4.2   COLORS AND COLORED IMAGES IN SOAP BUBBLES

To do this experiment you will need:
- old newspapers.
- bubble wand
- sunlight
- bubble-making solution

Stand on newspapers in front of a well-lighted window or door. The newspapers will prevent the bubble-making solution from falling on the floor and making it slippery. Dip the wand into the soapy solution and blow gently into the soap film to make the biggest bubble you can. When the bubble breaks away from the wand, catch it on the wand, as shown in Figure 33.

Look into the bubble. Can you see colors? If you look closely, you will also see images in the bubble. How do the images formed by light reflected from the front surface of the bubble differ from those formed by reflections from the rear surface?

Repeat the experiment several times so you can see

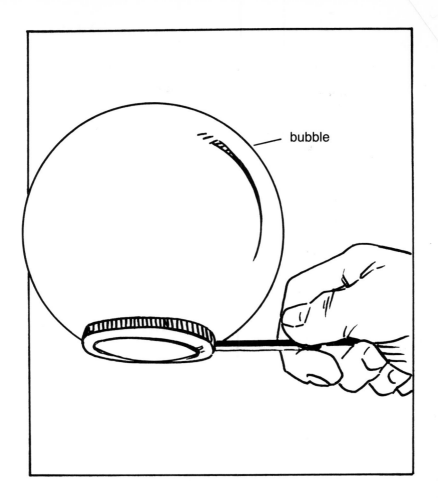

33) Catch a falling bubble!

PUZZLER 4.1
Why are the images formed by reflections from the front surface of the bubble right side up while those formed by reflections from the rear surface are up-side down?

the images clearly. Do the colors seen in the images change as the soap film in the bubble drains and becomes thinner?

4.3   REFLECTIONS, COLORS, AND THIN FILMS

To do this experiment you will need:
- old newspapers
- bubble wand
- water
- clear nail polish
- sunlight
- bubble-making solution
- large, shallow container

Stand with your back to a north well-lighted window. Dip a bubble wand into some bubble-making solution. Hold the wand in front of your face. Turn the wand slowly until you can see the colored bands that stretch across the thin soap film on the wand. What happens to these colored bands as the soap film drains? Can you see images formed by light reflected from the thin film? What do you see forming at the top of the film as the soap film drains?

Pour water into a large, shallow container. Place a small drop of clear nail polish on the water. The nail polish spreads out over the water like a drop of oil on a water-coated pavement. What colors can you see in light reflected from the coated surface of the water?

PUZZLER 4.2
Why do we see separate colors reflected from thin films such as soap films or oil on water?

4.4 REFLECTED COLORS AND THEIR MIXES

To do this experiment you will need:
- adult to help you
- red, green, and blue lightbulbs (most supermarkets carry colored bulbs)
- white wall
- 2 large sheets of cardboard
- 3 light sockets and cords or 3 study lamps

Ask an adult to help you with this experiment because you will be using electrical outlets. Place three light sockets near a white wall, as shown in Figure 34. Screw a blue lightbulb into the middle socket. Screw a red lightbulb into the socket on one side of the blue lightbulb and a green lightbulb into the socket on the other side.

Ask the adult to plug the cord from the blue lightbulb's socket into an electrical outlet. What color is the

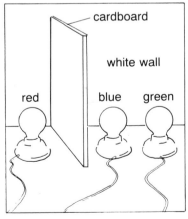

34) Mixing colored light.

light reflected from the wall? ***Have the adult*** turn off the blue lightbulb.

Repeat the experiment using light from only the red lightbulb. What color do you see reflected from the white wall?

Repeat the experiment using light from only the green lightbulb. What color do you see reflected from the white wall?

Mixing Blue and Red Light

Now turn off the green light and turn on the blue and red lightbulbs. Place a large sheet of cardboard between the lighted lightbulbs, as shown in Figure 34. The cardboard should extend to the wall so that you see red light reflected from the wall on one side of the cardboard and blue light on the other side. Pull the cardboard back away from the wall an inch or two so light from both lightbulbs can reach a small section of the wall. The color you see when both red and blue light are reflected to your eye is called magenta (ma-jen-ta). What would you have called it?

Mixing Green and Blue Light

Next, turn off the red lightbulb and place the cardboard between the lighted green and blue lightbulbs. Again, pull the cardboard back away from the wall slightly so light from both lightbulbs can reach a small section of the wall. The color you see when both green and blue light are reflected to your eye is called cyan (sigh-ann). What would you have called it?

Mixing Green and Red Light

Turn on all three lightbulbs. Place the cardboard between the red and blue lightbulbs. Then turn off the blue lightbulb and pull the cardboard back away from the wall a short way so light from the red and green lightbulbs can reach a small section of the wall. What color do you see when a mixture of red and green lights is reflected to your eye?

Mixing Blue, Green, and Red Light

Finally, with the cardboard between the red and blue lightbulbs, push one end of the cardboard against the wall. Turn on all three lightbulbs. You will see red on one side of the cardboard and cyan on the other side where the blue and green lights mix on the wall. Pull the cardboard back from the wall until you see a yellow band where red and green light overlap. Then pull the cardboard back another inch or two so light from all three bulbs can fall on a narrow strip of the wall. What color do you see when all three colors—red, blue, and green—are reflected to your eyes?

PUZZLER 4.3

What color will you see on each side of the cardboard if you place it between the blue and the red lightbulbs and push one end against the wall? When all three colors reach the wall, what color will you see?

Silvered mirrors were first made by the German chemist Justus von Liebig in 1835. He heated a solution of formaldehyde, ammonia, and silver nitrate beneath a sheet of glass. The silver vapors from the solution were deposited on the glass forming a reflective surface. A similar process is still used today to make most mirrors.

Reflections, Mirrors, and Science

Mirrors are one of the tools widely used by scientists. Astronomers use concave mirrors to produce images of the stars and planets. Biologists use mirrors to reflect light into microscopes. Much of modern communication and medicine depends on the total internal reflection of light in optical fibers made of glass.

Mirrors, Reflection, and Early Scientists

Sir Isaac Newton, perhaps the greatest scientist and mathematician who ever lived, invented the reflecting telescope. Newton used a concave mirror to reflect and converge light from stars, moons, and planets. The mirror was made of speculum metal—an alloy of

copper, tin, and arsenic—that Newton prepared him-
self. He placed a small plane mirror inside the barrel of
the telescope to reflect the converging light from the
concave mirror sideways to a lens where the light was
further converged to form an enlarged image (see Figure 35). Later, he used a small prism instead of the
plane mirror to reflect the converging light to a lens.

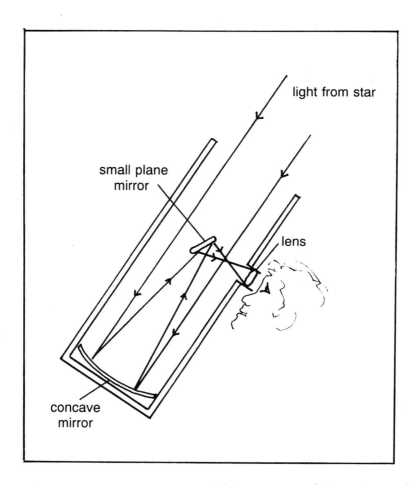

35) A diagram of Newton's reflecting telescope.

5.1   THE IMPORTANCE OF DIAMETER
IN A REFLECTING TELESCOPE

To do this experiment you will need:
- friend to help you
- concave mirror, such as the one you used in Experiment 2.2
- sheet of white cardboard
- black construction paper
- scissors
- well-lighted window

Newton's reflecting telescope measured only 15 centimeters (6 inches) in length, and the diameter of the concave mirror was only 2 centimeters (1 inch). You may have read about much larger reflecting telescopes and the great diameter of their main mirror. For example, the telescope at the Palomar Observatory in California has a diameter of 5.1 meters (16.7 feet).

To see why the diameter of the mirror is important, you will need a concave mirror, such as the one you used in Experiment 2.2, a sheet of white cardboard, and a sheet of black construction paper. Use scissors to cut a hole in the center of the construction paper. Make the diameter of the hole about one-third the diameter of the mirror.

Use the mirror to reflect light coming through a well-lighted window onto the cardboard screen held by a friend. Have your friend move the screen closer to, or farther from the mirror until the sharpest image possible appears on the screen. Now hold the black sheet with the hole in it against the mirror. What happens to the brightness of the image?

Remove the paper from the mirror. What happens to the image's brightness when you do this? What is the advantage of having a reflecting telescope with a large diameter?

Using Mirrors to Find the Speed of Light

During the nineteenth century, a number of scientists designed experiments to measure the speed of light. They knew that light traveled very fast, but they wanted to know exactly how fast it moved.

To find out, they would send a narrow beam of light over a large distance, reflect it back to its starting point, and measure the time it took for this to happen. Even over distances as large as 35.5 kilometers (20 miles), it took only about 0.0002 seconds for the light to travel the 71 kilometers (44 miles) to the mirror and back.

To measure such small intervals of time, Albert Michelson, an American physicist, used a rotating octagonal mirror like the one shown in Figure 36. He reflected a beam of light from one of the eight mirrors to a mirror 35.5 kilometers (22 miles) away. The reflected beam could be seen in a second mirror on the opposite side of the octagon, as shown. Michelson then used a motor to rotate the eight mirrors. At first, he could no longer see the reflected light. By the time the beam returned from the distant mirror, the rotating mirror had turned enough to deflect the beam along a different angle. But, Michelson thought, suppose the mirror was rotating fast enough so that it made 1/8th of a turn in the time it took the light to go to the distant mirror and back. In that case, the mirrors would be in exactly the same position they were when the octagon was not moving. The only difference would be that each mirror had replaced the one ahead of it. When the mirror was rotating 528 times per second, Michelson found the reflected beam became visible again. A mirror in the position from which the viewer could see the beam when the octagon was stationary had made one eighth of a turn, placing the next mirror in position to reflect the beam to the observer's eye. At higher rates of rotation the beam again disappeared. At 1,056 turns per second, the beam again became visible.

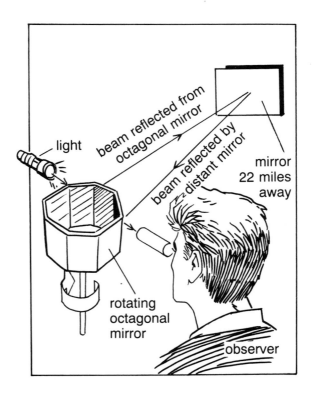

36) Michelson used a rotating octagonal mirror to measure the speed of light.

Now, the second mirror in the octagon was in position after one quarter of a turn of the octagon to reflect the beam to the observer. Michelson reasoned that if the octagon was turning 528 times per second, the time for each of the eight mirrors mounted on the octagon to make one eighth of a turn while the light traveled 44 miles must be:

1/8 x 1/528 seconds = 1/4224 seconds = 0.0002367 seconds

Thus, light traveled 71 kilometers (44 miles) in 0.0002367 seconds. Its speed, therefore, must be 71 kilometers (44 miles) per 0.0002367 second = 300,000 kilometers (186,000 miles) per second.

Michelson repeated the experiment over many different distances. The measurements always gave very nearly the same speed—300,000 kilometers (186,000 miles) per second . Michelson's experiment showed that the speed of light is constant; it does not depend on how far the light travels. It does, however, depend on the medium in which the light moves. In a vacuum, light travels at a speed of 300,000 kilometers per second. In air, its speed is almost the same, but in water the speed of light is 226,000 kilometers per second. The speed of light in glass is two-thirds its speed in air, or 200,000 kilometers per second.

Mirrors, Lasers, and the Distance to the Moon

During the late 1960s and early 1970s, astronauts landed on the moon. While there, they installed mirrors with reflecting surfaces that faced the earth. Later, lasers, which can produce a very narrow beam of light, were used to reflect pulses of light off the mirrors the astronauts had placed on the moon. By measuring the time it took a pulse of light to reach the moon and be reflected back to earth, astronomers could make accurate measurements of the distance to the moon.

These measurements, which confirmed less direct measurements, were carried out when the moon was at various places in its orbit about the earth. The shortest time for light pulses to go to the moon and back was found to be 2.32 seconds. The longest time was 2.66 seconds. Since light travels at a speed of 300,000 kilometers per second, astronomers could use the time measurements to determine the distance of the moon from the earth at perigee (when it is closest to earth) and apogee (when it is farthest from earth).

You use the same principle in estimating the distance to a destination you plan to reach by train. If the train moves at a steady speed of 50 miles per hour and it takes 2 hours to travel there, the destination is 100 miles away: 2 hours x 50 miles per hour = 100 miles.

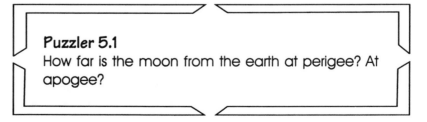

Puzzler 5.1
How far is the moon from the earth at perigee? At apogee?

Optic Fibers, Medicine, and Communication

As you saw in Chapter 3, all light inside glass will be reflected back into the glass if it strikes the surface at angles less than 42°. This principle, known as *total internal reflection,* is used extensively in medicine and communication.

To look at the inside of a patient's stomach, a doctor need not cut through the patient's body. Instead, he or she can use a pair of light pipes, each consisting of thousands of individual glass fibers. The flexible light pipes can be gently inserted through the patient's throat and esophagus (the tube that carries swallowed food) into his or her stomach. Light from outside the body is carried by the optic fibers in one pipe to the stomach. The light reflected from the stomach is carried back to the doctor's eye by a second light pipe.

Similar, but shorter, light pipes can be inserted into joints. In this way, surgeons can operate on knees and other joints after making a very small incision—one only large enough to insert the light pipe and surgical tool. The 10- to 15-centimeter (4- to 6-inch) incisions that used to be made in order to view and operate on a knee are no longer needed. As a result, recovery times are much shorter.

Optical fibers are also being used in communication. Light pulses can be sent along glass fibers just as electrical pulses can be transmitted by wires. However, much more information can be transmitted by glass fibers than by metal wires. For this reason, telephone and television wire cables are being replaced by cables made of optical fibers.

Expensive, front-surface mirrors are made by heating a metal such as aluminum in a vacuum. The vaporized metal condenses on a glass plate forming a smooth reflective layer.

Mirror Research

In this chapter you will have an opportunity to carry out some investigations that will give you more opportunity to do your own research. Some of these investigations will require new experiments. Some will require going to a library and/or talking to various people. Any conclusions you reach will be based on your own observations and measurements.

A Surprise following Experiment 6.1 will give you a chance to check up on your explanations for that experiment.

6.1   MIRROR IMAGES AND DISTANCE

To do this research you will need:
- pencil, paper, and protractor
- small plane mirror

Hold a small plane mirror close to your face. Look at your image in the mirror. Move the mirror until the image of the top of your head is at the top of the mirror. How much of your lower face is visible in the mirror? Can you see your eyes? Can you see your nose? Your lips? Your chin? Note the lowest part of your face that is visible when the top of your head is visible at the top of the mirror.

Now, move the mirror farther away. Again, adjust the mirror so that the image of the top of your head is at the top of the mirror. How much of your face is visible in the mirror now? Continue to move the mirror farther from your face. Does the portion of your face that you can see in the mirror change?

Tape the sides of the mirror to a door frame so that you can move farther than an arm's length from the mirror. (Be sure you don't cover the top or bottom of the mirror with tape!) Does the portion of your face that you can see in the mirror change?

Stand on one side of a room and face the wall. Hold the mirror close to your eyes. How much of the other side of the room can you see reflected in the mirror? Now move the mirror farther from your face. As the

SURPRISE 6.1
You may have been surprised to find that when the distance between you and a mirror increases, the portion of your face that is visible in the mirror does not change. However, the area behind you that is visible in the mirror diminishes as the mirror moves farther from you. How can you explain this surprise?

mirror is moved farther from your eyes, how much of the other side of the room is visible in the mirror? Does the portion of the room you can see increase or decrease as the distance between you and the mirror grows larger?

6.2   ANTIGRAVITY ILLUSIONS AND MIRAGES

To do this research you will need:
- full-length store display windows that form an outside corner
- large and small mirrors
- conditions needed for mirages

Antigravity illusions are easy and fun to make. Mirages, however, are more difficult to find or create. Given the right lighting (see Chapter 1), you can make an antigravity illusion using a full-length store display window next to a recessed doorway. Such windows are quite common. Stand so that half your body is hidden by the wall. If you stand on your hidden leg and raise your visible one, you and your reflected image will appear to be suspended above the ground when viewed by someone at the other end of the window (see Figure 37).

Using large mirrors or store windows, see how many antigravity illusions you can create. What other illusions can you create using mirrors? How do magicians use mirrors to create illusions?

Light Refracted by Air
Many people think that mirages are the result of reflected light. Actually, mirages are caused by light that

is bent (refracted) as it passes through air. For example, light passing from cool to warm air (or warm to cool air) is bent. The bending is not sudden, as it is when light passes from air to water (or water to air), but is gradual and depends on temperature differences in the air. Nevertheless, the light reaching your eye may appear to be coming from some place other than its real source. Perhaps you have seen a mirage while driving on a long straight highway on a hot day. Far ahead, the highway may have appeared to be covered with

37) Creating an antigravity illusion.

water. Yet, when you reach that distant part of the road, there is nothing but dry, hot pavement. What you saw was light from the sky along the horizon. As the light approached the hot air above the pavement, it was bent upward. Therefore, you saw the sky on the road ahead. The skylight on the road looked like water.

Mirages over Water

You can sometimes see mirages by looking across a large body of water such as a bay or a lake. If the water is much cooler than the air above it, light coming from a warm, distant shore line may be bent downward. This causes the shore line to appear elevated above the water leaving a gap between the water and the land.

Look for mirages like the ones described. They are common in deserts, hot plains, and over large bodies of water. Knowing the circumstances that cause mirages, you can look for smaller mirages. You may find them or test for them along long walls heated by the sun, on hot sandy beaches, along ice-covered lakes beneath spring-like air, and so on.

6.3   ANOTHER RAINBOW

To do this research you will need:
- small plane mirror
- white screen (white cardboard or white paper taped to cardboard)
- dish
- water
- sunlight

Using a small rectangular mirror and a dish of water to represent raindrops, sunlight, and a white screen, see if you can produce a rainbowlike band of light on the screen. Remember what you learned about rainbows in Experiment 4.1.

6.4 MIRRORS AND VOCATIONS

You have already seen how astronomers use mirrors in telescopes (Chapter 5). How do dentists use a mirror in their profession? How do truck drivers and experienced drivers use mirrors when they back up their vehicles? In what other professions do people use mirrors to carry out their work? How do they use them?

6.5 REFLECTIONS IN PHOTOGRAPHS

Examine a photograph of reflected images seen in a lake or pond. Turn the photograph upside down. Is there any way to tell whether the photo is right side up or upside down?

6.6 REFLECTED LIGHT AND THE MOON

To do this research you will need:
- place where you can observe the moon
- materials to make a model of the moon's phases

Unlike the sun, the moon's appearance changes from night to night. Is moonlight emitted by the moon or is it sunlight reflected from the moon to the earth? Why does the moon's appearance change in a predictable way during the course of a month? Design a model to explain the phases (changes) of the moon.

On a few days each month following a new moon, you can observe a thin sliver of moon—a crescent moon. It is visible in the western sky shortly after sunset on these days. Look closely at a crescent moon. In addition to the bright crescent, you can also observe that the rest of the moon is faintly visible. What is the source of light that makes the rest of the moon faintly visible?

6.7 MIRRORS AT RIGHT ANGLES

To do this research you will need:
- 2 large mirrors at right angles to one another
- comb
- pencil and paper

Find a room where two large mirrors are at right angles to one another. (Many bathrooms have mirrors arranged in this way.) If you can't find such a place, find two large mirrors and **ask an adult** to help you find a way to support them upright at right angles.

As you found in Experiment 3.1, you can see three images of yourself in the mirrors. Look at the center image—the one that is formed by light that has been reflected twice. While looking at this image, try to comb your hair. Why do you think it is so difficult to do? Is it easier to write a message while looking into the mirror? Can you read the message by looking into the mirror?

6.8   YOU AND A MIRROR

To do this research you will need:
- mirrors of different sizes
- pencil or pen
- yardstick or ruler
- paper or notebook

How is the portion of you that you can see in a mirror related to the size of the mirror? For example, if you have a mirror 30 centimeters (1 foot) tall, how many feet (or inches) of your height can you see in the mirror? While you look into a mirror, have someone with a yardstick or ruler measure the portion of your height that you can see in the mirror. Repeat the experiment with mirrors of various sizes. Record your results on a piece of paper or in a notebook.

Is there any relationship between the height of the mirror and the portion of your height that you can see in the mirror? Do you need a mirror as tall as you are to see your entire height?

Answers to Puzzlers and Surprises

Puzzler 1.1

Light paths are straight and reversible. If light can travel from A to B to C, as shown in Figure 38a, it can also travel from C to B to A.

Light travels in straight lines. If you stand behind the plane of a mirror, light reflected from you will never reach the reflecting surface of the mirror. There will be

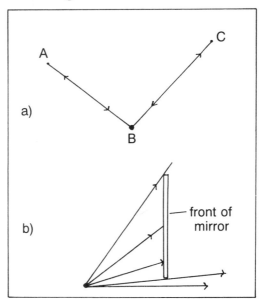

38a) Light rays are straight and reversible.

b) If you are behind a mirror, no light from you can reach the mirror's reflecting surface.

no image of you until you, or some part of you, is in front of the plane of the mirror (Figure 38b.)

Puzzler 1.2
Light on either side of the shadow is reflected, which makes it appear as though the shadow itself is reflected.

Surprise 1.1
The reflected beam becomes more and more circular the farther it travels, regardless of the shape of the mirror used to reflect the beam. A similar effect can be seen if you make pinhole images of the sun. Use a pin to make a small hole near the center of a piece of black construction paper. If you hold the paper in a beam of sunlight, you can see an image of the sun on a piece of white cardboard held below the pinhole as shown in Figure 39a.

Now fold the paper in half and use scissors to make tiny square, triangular, and rectangular holes in the paper (see Figure 39b) beside the pinhole. If you hold the black paper close to the screen, the light beams coming through the holes will have the same shape as the holes. As you move the paper toward the sun and farther from the screen, you will find that all the beams seen on the screen become circular.

A square mirror acts like a large square hole. Instead of simply transmitting a narrow beam of sunlight the way a hole does, a mirror reflects a narrow beam. Both beams become circles because both form images of the sun.

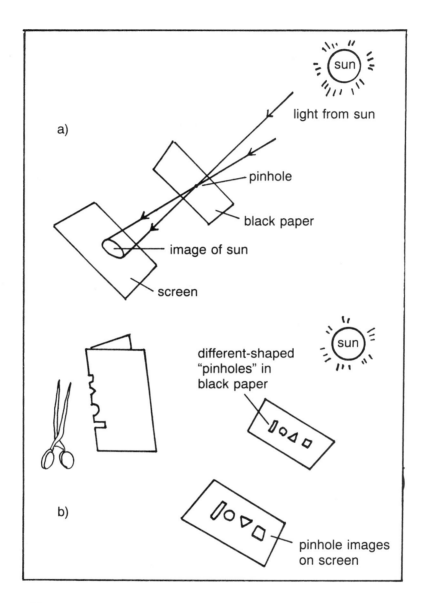

a)

light from sun

pinhole

black paper

image of sun

screen

different-shaped
"pinholes" in
black paper

b)

pinhole images
on screen

39a) Pinhole image of the sun.

b) Cut tiny square, rectangular, and triangular holes beside the pinhole. Use them to make "pinhole" images.

Puzzler 1.3

Light reflects from both the front and rear surface of the glass pane. Because more light reflects from the front surface of the glass, the image that is nearest your finger is the brighter one. The second (fainter) image is reflected from the rear surface and, therefore, is farther from your finger. With two glass panes separated by an air space, there are four images, two for each glass.

A front surface mirror or a shiny metal has only one reflecting surface; consequently, only one image is formed. With a rear surface mirror, the back side of the glass is coated with silver, which is a strong reflector. Some reflection occurs on the front glass surface as well. Because the glass is not as good a reflector as silver, the front surface image—the one that touches your finger—is the fainter image.

Puzzler 1.4

Experiment 1.11 uses only two of the many light rays that come from a point on an object. In this case the object is a point on the flashlight bulb. In the case of real objects, every point on the object sends out countless rays. But the principle is the same. The rays that strike the mirror are reflected to form an image. The two diverging rays of light in Experiment 1.11 appear to be coming from a point behind the mirror. Rays from other points on the object would reflect so as to appear to be coming from slightly different points behind the mirror. All the reflected rays together produce an image that is a clear likeness of the object. As you saw in Experiment

1.5, these rays appear to come from an image that is as far behind the mirror as the object is in front.

Puzzler 1.5

A white card feels smooth, but compared with a mirror it is really quite rough. Consequently, it may reflect light rays that are close together in very different directions as shown in Figure 40. A mirror's very smooth surface reflects any narrow light beam in only one direction, not many. It is the uniform reflection of light from a mirror that enables it to form clear images.

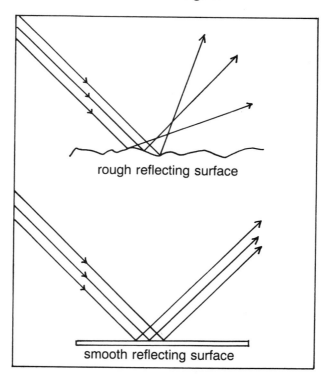

rough reflecting surface

smooth reflecting surface

40) A rough surface reflects light rays that are close together in very different directions. A smooth surface reflects them in a very regular way.

Puzzler 2.1
The greater the convexity (curvature) of the mirror, the smaller the images.

Puzzler 2.2
Light from distant objects that strikes a concave mirror is converged. This makes it possible to bring light rays from a point on an object back together again. Plane and convex mirrors cannot make light converge.

Surprise 2.1
Images formed in your eye persist (remain) for about a twentieth of a second. If the stick is moved up and down fast enough, the parts of the image that you see when the stick is at various positions persist long enough for you to see the entire image. Similar phenomena take place on movie and television screens.

Puzzler 2.3
The front surface of the lens acts like a convex mirror; the rear surface acts like a concave mirror. Each surface reflects some light and forms an image of the candle flame. Only the rear (concave) surface can bring light rays together to form a real image as you found in Experiment 2.3.

Surprise 3.1
As you can see by studying Figure 41a, light rays from the top and bottom of an object are switched and reverse direction because of the double reflection. This is not the case if the light rays continue in the same direction as shown in Figure 41b.

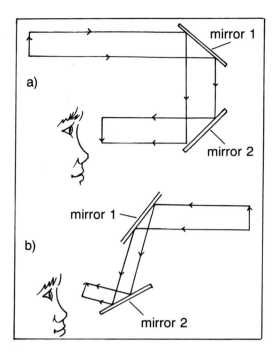

41a) Images from objects in back of you are turned upsidedown by double reflection.

b) Objects in front of you are not turned upsidedown by double reflection.

Puzzler 3.1

Figure 42a shows how double reflection of light from a face between the mirrors produces an upside-down image. Figure 42b shows how double reflection produces an image in which the image's right is the object's right and the image's left is the object's left. This is what you might expect from the image of an image.

Puzzler 3.2

Each time the light is reflected, a new image is produced. With parallel mirrors, there is no end to the

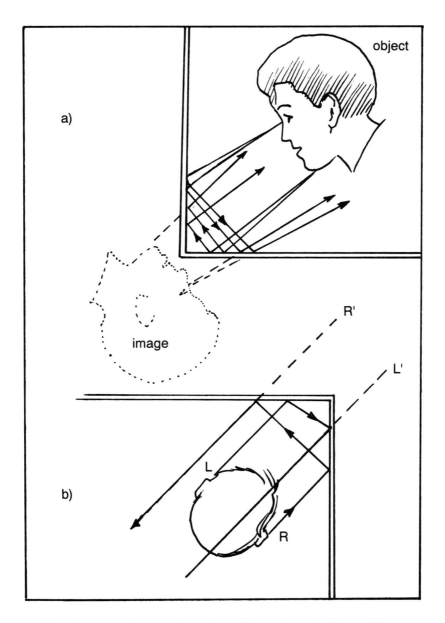

42a) Double reflections from the mirrors shown in Figure 22a produce an upside-down image.

b) Double reflections from the mirrors shown in Figure 22b produce an image in which the image's right is the object's right.

number of reflections that can occur. However, some light is absorbed and the image becomes smaller each time the light is reflected. After many reflections, the image finally becomes too faint or too small to be seen.

Surprise 3.2
See Experiment 3.6.

Puzzler 3.3
All light from the coin striking the glass at angles less than 42° from the glass surface will be totally reflected back into the water as shown in Figure 43. If your eye is at position 1, no light from the coin will be visible. At position 2 or 2', you can see the coin because the light that was totally reflected emerges through the water's surface. The points where these light rays seem to come from produces the image you see.

Puzzler 3.4
The image that points toward the mirror is formed by light that passes from your finger to the mirror and back to your eye. The image that points away from the mirror is formed by light that passes from your finger to the surface of the water where it is reflected to the mirror and then to your eye.

Puzzler 4.1
Some of the light that strikes the front surface of the bubble is reflected. Since this surface is convex, the images are similar to those formed by a convex mirror;

they are right side up. The rear surface of the mirror has a concave surface; therefore, light reflected from it behaves as if it were coming from a concave mirror, which can form upside-down images.

Puzzler 4.2

With very thin films, the color of the light that is reflected depends on the thickness of the film. At one

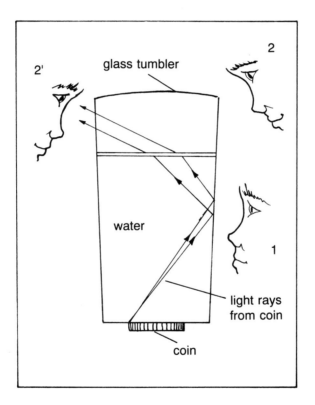

43) At position 1 the coin can't be seen because all the light from the coin is reflected back into the water. At position 2 or 2' the light from the coin that was reflected back into the water can be seen after it emerges through the water's surface.

thickness, blue light may be reflected. At a slightly different thickness green light will be reflected and so on. As a result, you see different colored bands in a draining soap film because the film gradually becomes thinner at the top and thicker at the bottom. When the film is very thin (about a millionth of an inch thick), we see no reflected light; the film appears black.

Puzzler 4.3

As you can see for yourself, the wall in front of the red lightbulb is red; the wall in front of the blue and green lightbulbs is cyan. All three colors will produce white.

Puzzler 5.1

At perigee, it takes 2.32 seconds for light to go to the moon and back. Since light travels through space at a speed of 300,000 kilometers per second, the distance it travels in 2.32 seconds is:

> 2.32 seconds x 300,000 kilometers per second = 696,000 kilometers (435,000 miles)

> But this is to the moon and back. The distance to the moon would be half as far or 348,000 kilometers (217,500 miles).

At apogee the distance would be:

> (2.66 seconds x 300,000 kilometers ÷ 2) = 399,000 kilometers (249,000 miles)

Surprise 6.1

No matter where you stand in front of a mirror, the portion of you that is visible to your eye remains the same. As you move farther from the mirror (from position 1 to 2 in Figure 44a), the light ray with the largest incident angle that can reach the mirror from you grows (from x to x'). Similarly, the angle of reflection grows from y to y'. But the distance between the origin of these two incident rays (the height of you visible in the mirror) remains the same. If you draw the reflected rays from eye to mirror carefully for yourself, and then draw the incident rays that gave rise to them for different eye positions, you will see that the height of you that is visible is always the same.

On the other hand, as your eye moves closer to a mirror (Figure 44b), the cone of rays that can reach your eye from the area behind you grows larger.

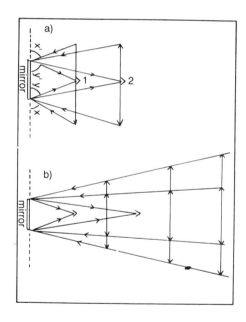

44a) Whether at position 1 or 2, the portion of yourself that you can see is the same.

   b) The farther away the background, the more of it that falls within the cone of light that can reach your eye. The farther your eye is from the mirror, the smaller that cone becomes.

Further Reading

Anderson, L. W. *Light and Color*. Milwaukee: Raintree, 1988.

Ardley, Neil. *Sun and Light*. New York: Watts, 1983.

Berger, Melvin. *Simple Science Says: Take One Mirror*. New York: Scholastic, 1989.

Broekel, Ray. *Experiments with Light*. Chicago: Childrens Press, 1986.

Catherall, Ed. *Exploring Light*. Austin, Tex.: Steck-Vaughn, 1990.

Gardner Robert. *Science Around the House*. New York: Messner, 1987.

Gardner, Robert, and David Webster. *Science in Your Backyard*. New York: Messner, 1987.

Orii, Eiji and Masako. *Simple Science Experiments with Light*. Milwaukee: Gareth Stevens, 1989.

Seymour, Simon. *Mirror Magic*. New York: Lothrop, 1980.

Taylor, Barbara. *Shadows and Reflections*. New York: Warwick, 1990.

Walpole, Brenda. *Light*. New York: Warwick, 1987.

Zubrowski, Bernie. *Mirrors: Finding Out About the Properties of Light*. Morrow, 1992.

Index

Kitty Coleman

I woke this morning with a stranger in my bed. The head of blond hair beside me was decidedly not my husband's. I did not know whether to be shocked or amused.

Well, I thought, here's a novel way to begin the new century.

Then I remembered the evening before and felt rather sick. I wondered where Richard was in this huge house and how we were meant to swap back. Everyone else here—the man beside me included—was far more experienced in the mechanics of these matters than I. Than we. Much as Richard bluffed last night, he was just as much in the dark as me, though he was more keen. Much more keen. It made me wonder.

I nudged the sleeper with my elbow, gently at first and then harder until at last he woke with a snort.

"Out you go," I said. And he did, without a murmur. Thankfully he didn't try to kiss me. How I stood that beard last night I'll never remember—the claret helped, I suppose. My cheeks are red with scratches.

When Richard came in a few minutes later, clutching his clothes in a bundle, I could barely look at him. I was embarrassed, and angry too—angry that I should feel embarrassed and yet not expect him to feel so as well. It was all the more infuriating that he simply kissed me, said, "Hello, darling," and began to dress. I could smell her perfume on his neck.

Yet I could say nothing. As I myself have so often said, I am open minded—I pride myself on it. Those words bite now.

I lay watching Richard dress, and found myself thinking of my brother. Harry always used to tease me for thinking too much—though he refused to concede that he was at all responsible for encouraging me. But all those evenings spent reviewing with me what his tutors had taught him in the morning—he said it was to help him remember it—what did that do but teach me to think and speak my mind? Perhaps he regretted it later. I shall never know now. I am only just out of mourning for him, but some days it feels as if I am still clutching that telegram.

Harry would be mortified to see where his teaching has led. Not that one has to be clever for this sort of thing—most of them downstairs are stupid as buckets of coal, my blond beard among them. Not one could I have a proper conversation with—I had to resort to the wine.

Frankly I'm relieved not to be of this set—to paddle in its shallows occasionally is quite enough for me. Richard I suspect feels differently, but he has married the wrong wife if he wanted that sort of life. Or perhaps it is I who chose badly—though I would never have thought so once, back when we were mad for each other.

I think Richard has made me do this to show me he is not as conventional as I feared. But it has had the opposite effect on me. He has become everything I had not thought he would be when we married. He has become ordinary.

I feel so flat this morning. Daddy and Harry would have laughed at me, but I secretly hoped that the change in the century would bring a change in us all; that England would miraculously slough off her shabby black coat to reveal something glittering and new. It is only eleven hours into the twentieth century, yet I know very well that nothing has changed but a number.

Enough. They are to ride today, which is not for me—I shall escape with my coffee to the library. It will undoubtedly be empty.